Table of Contents

Executive Summary

The National Credit Union Administration is pleased to transmit the Second Annual Report to Congress on Minority Depository Institutions for the reporting period of July 1, 2013, through June 30, 2014. The report is submitted pursuant to Section 367 of the Dodd-Frank Wall Street Reform and Consumer Protection Act (Dodd-Frank Act) which requires NCUA to dedicate efforts toward preserving and encouraging minority depository institutions. NCUA is also required to document its efforts to achieve the policy goals set forth in Section 367 of the Dodd-Frank Act. Additionally, this report contains analyses of the composition and financial performance of minority depository institutions during this same time period.

As of June 30, 2014, NCUA supervised 688 minority depository institutions, representing nearly 11 percent of all federally insured credit unions. These minority-owned and managed credit unions play a vital role in their communities because they are frequently the only federally insured institutions serving low-to-moderate income, underserved, and unbanked populations. Otherwise, low-to-moderate income consumers and businesses would have to use non-traditional venues, such as payday lenders, check cashers, pawn shops and title loans to address their financial needs. As a result, these minority depository institutions play a vital role in meeting the financial needs of growing populations of minorities, such as Hispanic Americans and Asian Americans, and historically underserved communities, such as Black Americans.

Recognizing the importance of minority depository institutions and the unique challenges they often face in serving their communities, NCUA is taking proactive steps toward preserving and encouraging minority depository institutions through its Office of Minority and Women Inclusion. Established in January 2011, OMWI is charged with the responsibility of establishing and administering a program to preserve and encourage new minority depository institutions regulated by NCUA. NCUA is also in the process of finalizing the proposed Minority Depository Institution Preservation Program Interpretative Ruling and Policy Statement, outlining the agency's initiatives to preserve minority depository institutions.

During the reporting period, NCUA took several actions to preserve minority depository institutions, including:

- NCUA's Office of Small Credit Union Initiatives provided minority depository institutions with technical assistance, training, educational programs, videos, webinars, publications and other educational tools.

- NCUA's examiners of minority depository institutions:
  - provided assistance and guidance on examination and compliance issues between examination and supervision contacts;
  - facilitated the establishment of mentor relationships between credit unions; and
  - assisted in locating new sponsors for field of membership expansions and negotiating financial support to sustain minority depository institutions.

- NCUA's Office of Consumer Protection:
  - provided guidance to groups establishing new minority depository institutions;
  - assisted minority depository institutions with providing access to financial services by expanding their fields of membership;
  - issued a new credit union charter, a community conversion and low-income designations to increase capacity of minority depository institutions; and
  - developed webinars and other tools to provide education on consumer compliance regulatory issues and financial literacy.

In addition, NCUA is developing systems to track and monitor actions taken to preserve minority depository institutions. With these new systems, NCUA will be able to document and report on the steps the agency is taking to ensure minority depository institutions receive the needed technical assistance, training, educational programs, mentoring, chartering and other resources to flourish.

Minority Depository Institution Preservation Program

The NCUA Board issued the proposed Minority Depository Institution Preservation Program Interpretive Ruling and Policy Statement 13-1 along with a request for comments in July 2013. The policy statement details the program's proposed objectives for preserving and encouraging minority depository institutions, consistent with NCUA's mission and strategic goal of ensuring a safe, sound and sustainable credit union system. NCUA is in the process of finalizing this policy statement.

The proposed policy statement defines the term "minority depository institution" and highlights the program's features. To qualify as a minority depository institution in the proposed policy statement, a federally insured credit union's percentage of both minority members and minority senior leadership must each exceed 50 percent. To identify an eligible minority group, NCUA relies upon the definition of a "minority" found in Section 308 of the Financial Institutions Reform, Recovery, and Enforcement Act of 1989. This definition includes any "Black American, Asian American, Hispanic American, or Native American."

As of June 30, 2014, approximately 688 credit unions self-certified as meeting the minority depository institution criteria using NCUA's Credit Union Online Profile system. This number represents a decline from the preceding year and is largely due to further clarification of the minority depository institution eligibility criteria in the policy statement and the self-certification process in the Credit Union Online Profile System.

Minority Depository (Credit Union) Institutions

A credit union is a member-owned and controlled, not-for-profit cooperative financial institution formed to permit groups of people to save, borrow and obtain financial services and participate in its management. The member ownership and control make credit unions unique.

For this reason, minority ownership is defined by the minority composition of the credit union's membership, as well as the minority composition of its senior leadership.[1] NCUA's Office of Minority and Women Inclusion will administer the Minority Depository Institution Preservation Program. The office is responsible for encouraging diversity, at all levels, within NCUA and the credit union system in accordance with Section 342 of the Dodd-Frank Act.

NCUA regulated 688 federally insured credit unions that qualify as minority depository institutions as of June 30, 2014. These institutions represent 10.7 percent of all federally insured credit unions. A complete listing of minority depository institutions regulated by NCUA can be found in Appendix 1.

The distribution of these institutions by racial or ethnic representation is shown in the table below.

	Number of Credit Unions	Percent MDIs	Total Assets	Average Assets	Total Members
Black American	343	50%	$5,833,432,480	$17,007,092	871,157
Hispanic American	118	17%	$9,910,703,921	$83,989,016	1,285,269
Asian American*	56	8%	$4,534,681,687	$80,976,459	362,637
Native American	13	2%	$133,449,634	$10,265,356	33,179
Multi-Cultural**	158	23%	$16,494,894,375	$104,398,066	1,984,541
Total Minority Depository Institutions	688	100%	$36,907,162,097	$53,644,131	4,536,783
Total Federally Insured Credit Unions	6,429		$1,103,309,333,546	$171,614,455	98,017,167

*Asian Americans include Native Hawaiian and Other Pacific Islanders.
**Multi-Cultural is two or more racial backgrounds at the same minority depository institution, such as Black Americans and Hispanic Americans.

---

[1] Senior leadership includes the members of the credit union's board of directors, credit and supervisory committees, and senior management staff, such as the CEO or manager, assistant manager, and chief financial and operations officers.

The 688 minority depository institutions have total assets of $36.9 billion, and are owned by 4.5 million members. The total assets of minority depository institutions represent 3.3 percent of total assets in all federally insured credit unions. The 4.5 million members who own these minority depository institutions represent 4.6 percent of the total members of federally insured credit unions.

Geographic Concentrations of Minority Depository Institutions

The map below shows the geographic locations and the concentrations of the 688 minority depository institutions as of June 30, 2014.

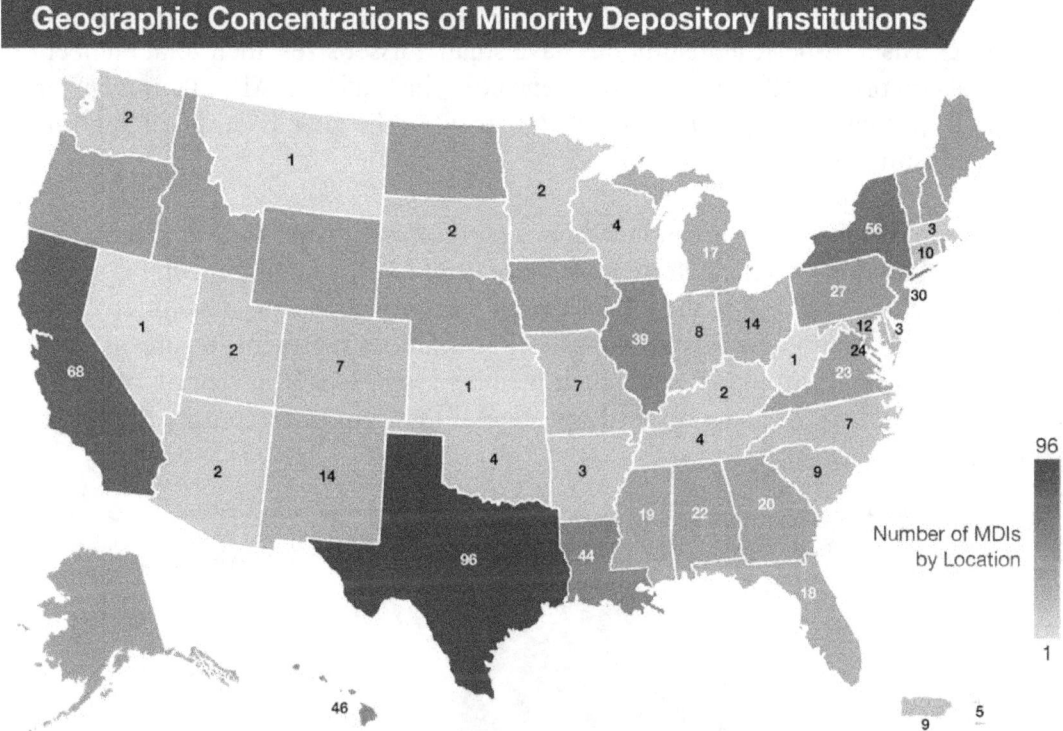

States with the highest concentration of minority depository institutions are Texas with 96 institutions, California with 68 institutions, New York with 56 institutions, Hawaii with 46 institutions, Louisiana with 44 institutions, and Illinois with 39 institutions.

States or U.S. territories with no minority depository institutions (shaded in brown) include Alaska, Idaho, Iowa, Maine, Nebraska, New Hampshire, North Dakota, Oregon, Rhode Island, Vermont, Wyoming and Guam (not pictured).

Composition of Minority Depository Institutions

The minority depository institutions' asset sizes, total members and distribution percentages remained relatively constant since last year. When excluding the Multi-Cultural institutions, the Hispanic American and Asian American institutions continue to represent the majority of deposits in minority depository institutions according to their average asset sizes. The average total assets are approximately $84 million for Hispanic American institutions and $81 million for Asian American institutions. The Black American and Native American institutions still have the smallest asset sizes as evidenced by their average total assets of approximately $17 and $10 million, respectively.

Even though Black American institutions have smaller asset sizes, their total number of institutions comprises half of all minority depository institutions. Also, their members represent 19 percent of total members and 16 percent of the total assets in all minority depository institutions.

The number of Hispanic American institutions represents 17 percent of total minority depository institutions, while their members represent 28 percent of all members and total assets equal 27 percent of the total assets of minority depository institutions. The number of Asian American minority depository institutions represents 8 percent of all minority depository institutions, while their members represent 8 percent of total membership and their assets represent 12 percent of total assets of minority depository institutions.

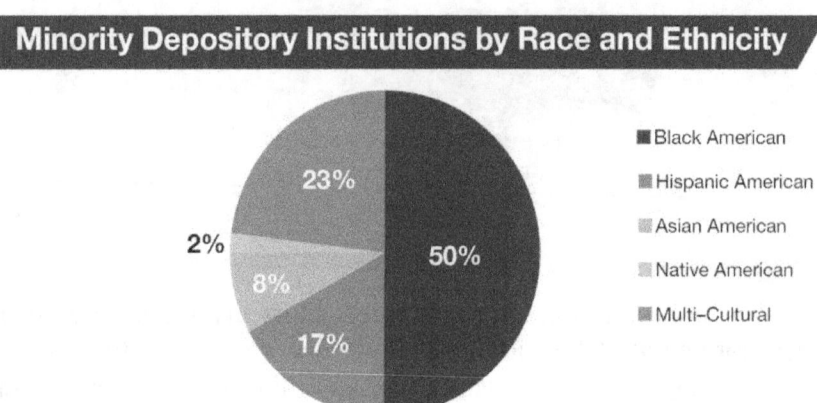

The number of Multi-Cultural institutions, which consists of institutions owned by two or more racial or ethnic cultures, equals 23 percent of all minority depository institutions. Their total assets, averaging $104 million, comprise the majority of total assets in all minority depository institutions. Their members represent 44 percent of all members and their total assets represent 45 percent of total assets in all minority depository institutions.

The following chart illustrates the percentage of total minority depository institutions within certain asset ranges.

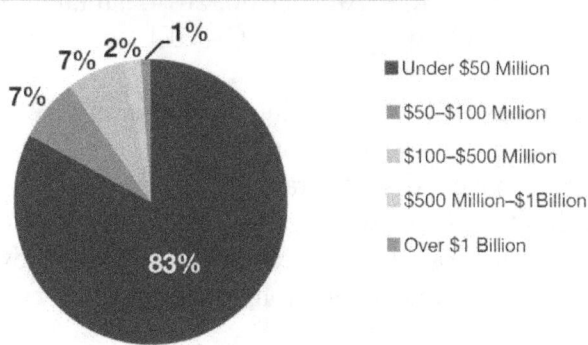

Minority Depository Institutions by Asset Size

7% 7% 2% 1%

83%

- Under $50 Million
- $50–$100 Million
- $100–$500 Million
- $500 Million–$1 Billion
- Over $1 Billion

Most minority depository institutions (83 percent) have total assets of $50 million or less, which is significantly higher than the credit union system overall, in which approximately two-thirds of federally insured credit unions have less than $50 million in assets. Approximately 7 percent of minority depository institutions have total assets ranging from $50 million to $100 million, while another 7 percent have assets of $100 million to $500 million. Due to the minority depository institutions' small asset sizes, most are challenged by the lack of sufficient resources, which demonstrates their need for technical assistance and assistance in expanding their operations, services and fields of membership.

Key Financial Indicators

Overall, minority depository institutions are financially sound. Most have satisfactory CAMEL composite ratings and adequate net worth ratios. NCUA uses both measurements as key indicators of federally insured credit unions' safety and soundness.

CAMEL Ratings
CAMEL is NCUA's internal rating system used for evaluating the soundness of credit unions on a uniform basis, determining the degree of risk to the National Credit Union Share Insurance Fund, and identifying those credit unions requiring special supervisory attention or concern. The system is based upon an evaluation of five critical elements of a credit union's operations: capital adequacy, asset quality, management, earnings, and liquidity/asset-liability management.

In composite and component CAMEL ratings, a rating of 1 is the best and a rating of 5 means a credit union has severe to significant weakness.

The composite CAMEL rating for the vast majority of minority depository institutions continues to be 3 or better. As of June 30, 2014, a total of 594 institutions, or 86 percent, fall into the following range of CAMEL composite ratings:

- 6 percent have a CAMEL rating of 1, meaning they are sound in every respect and any weaknesses are minor.
- 41 percent have a CAMEL rating of 2, meaning they are fundamentally sound and exhibit moderate weaknesses.
- 39 percent have a CAMEL rating of 3, meaning they exhibit a combination of weaknesses that may range from moderate to severe.

A total of 94 minority depository institutions are CAMEL codes 4 or 5. These troubled credit unions represent 14 percent of all minority depository institutions.

The following chart shows a comparison of the percentage of minority depository institutions by composite CAMEL ratings as of June 30, 2013 and June 30, 2014.

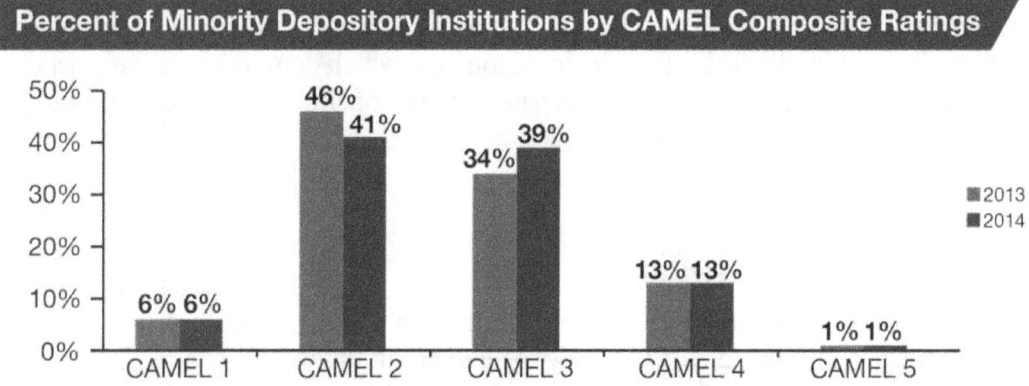

Minority depository institutions primarily shifted from a composite CAMEL rating of 2 in 2013 to a composite CAMEL rating of 3 in 2014.

Net Worth
Net worth is defined as the balance of the credit union's retained earnings at quarter-end, as determined under generally accepted accounting principles. Retained earnings consist of undivided earnings, regular reserves and any other appropriations designated by management or regulatory authorities.

The majority of the minority depository institutions have strong capital positions, which enhances their ability to sustain unknown losses and maintain their economic viability. The average net worth for all minority depository institutions was 15.35 percent, while the average net worth for all federally insured credit unions was 10.77 percent as of June 30, 2014.

According to the June 30, 2014, Call Report data, 95.4 percent of all minority depository institutions are considered, by statute, to be well-capitalized with a net worth ratio of 7 percent or above, and 3.2 percent are adequately capitalized with a net worth of 6.00–6.99 percent. However, the remaining 1.4 percent of minority depository institutions are undercapitalized as follows:

- 0.7 percent are undercapitalized reflecting a net worth ratio of 4.00–5.99 percent.
- 0.4 percent are significantly undercapitalized reflecting a net worth ratio of 2.00–3.99 percent.
- 0.3 percent are critically undercapitalized reflecting a net worth ratio of less than 2 percent.

Most credit unions that are undercapitalized are subject to Prompt Corrective Action, as prescribed in Part 702 of NCUA's Rules and Regulations. The regulation establishes mandatory and discretionary supervisory actions, including the development and implementation of a viable Net Worth Restoration Plan that is designed to return the credit union to a sound financial condition.

The chart below shows the net worth in minority depository institutions has slightly improved since June 30, 2013.

Net Worth in Minority Depository Institutions 2013 vs. 2014

2013

2014

2%   98%   1%   99%

■ Well or Adequately Capitalized

■ Undercapitalized

Return on Average Assets

Net income is the revenue remaining after covering all operating costs. The return on average assets is the ratio of net income to average total assets, which measures the efficiency of an institution using its assets to generate net income.

As of June 30, 2014, the average return on assets ratio among all minority depository institutions was 0.59 percent, compared to the average return on assets ratio of 0.81 percent for all federally insured credit unions. The primary reason for the smaller return on assets in minority depository institutions is their higher overall operating expenses.

Based on the June 30, 2014, Call Report data, most minority depository institutions (65 percent) are earning sufficient revenue to cover their operating costs, as shown in the chart below.

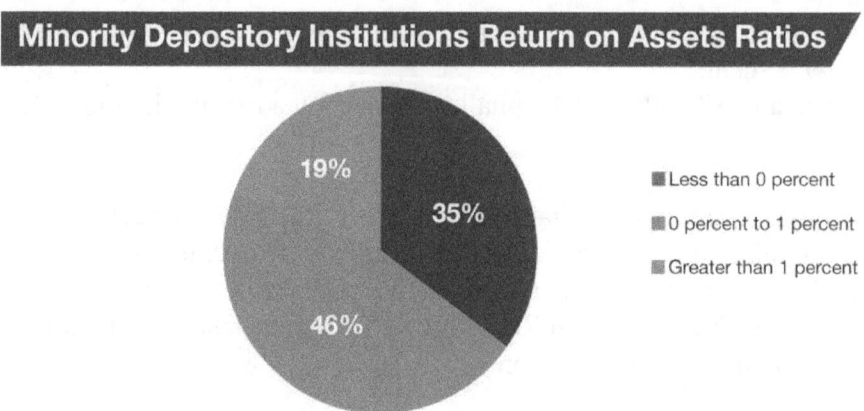

Of the 449 minority depository institutions experiencing positive return on assets ratios, or net earnings, 314 institutions (46 percent) are achieving net earnings of zero to one percent of average assets, while 135 institutions (19 percent) are achieving net earnings greater than one percent of average assets. These net earnings strengthen capital positions and sustain operations.

The remaining 239 institutions (35 percent) are experiencing challenges in meeting operating costs. These institutions generally experience higher expenses related to problem loans, overhead and products and services. Minority depository institutions have an average operating expenses-to-gross income ratio of 113.22 percent, compared to 66.47 percent for all federally insured credit unions as of June 30, 2014.

This demonstrates minority depository institutions' need for monetary assistance in funding operations and providing needed products and services while achieving sufficient profitability. Therefore, examiners and economic development specialists will continue to guide officials on ways to increase revenue, reduce operating expenses or some combination of both.[2]

Finally, through the Community Development Revolving Loan Fund, NCUA provides grants and loans to low-income designated credit unions, some of which are minority depository institutions, to help these credit unions develop new products and services. The agency also offers grants to help low-income designated credit unions become certified as Community Development Financial Institutions, thereby enabling them to access funding through initiatives sponsored by the U.S. Treasury.

Loan Delinquency

The loan delinquency ratio represents the portion of an institution's loan portfolio that is delinquent from missed loan payments. The chart below shows the majority of minority depository institutions have loan delinquency ratios in excess of 1 percent.

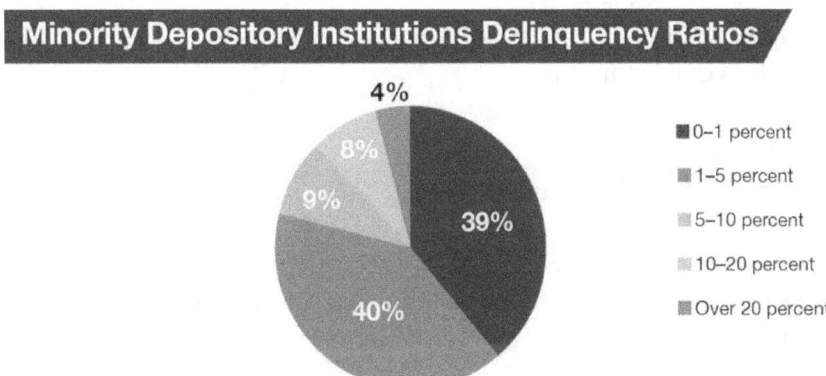

A total of 418 minority depository institutions (or 60 percent) have loan delinquency ratios in excess of 1 percent. The average loan delinquency ratio for all minority depository institutions was 4.24 percent, while the average loan delinquency ratio was 0.85 percent for all federally insured credit unions as of June 30, 2014. Institutions serving low-to-moderate income individuals generally experience higher levels of delinquent loans than other financial depository institutions.

Approximately 68 percent of the minority depository institutions have low-income designations representing membership that predominantly lives in low-to-moderate income zip codes. Often, these individuals use nontraditional sources to meet their

---

[2] Economic development specialists work in NCUA's Office of Small Credit Union Initiatives. They are dedicated to providing consulting and technical assistance to credit unions involved in the office's programs.

financial needs. These statistics illustrate the need for additional financial literacy education.

Financial Literacy Initiatives

NCUA will continue to work with minority depository institutions to assist them in providing financial literacy training to their members.

NCUA's financial literacy initiatives provide personal finance resources to credit unions and their members. Examples of these resources include:

- The consumer website, MyCreditUnion.gov, and its financial literacy focused microsite Pocket Cents, feature easy to use, personal finance educational information, tools, and resources. The website is also available in Spanish. Some featured webpages are:
  - Paying off Credit Cards
  - Dealing with Debt
  - Protecting your Finances
  - Buying a Car
  - Credit Reports and Credit Scores
  - Financial Tools and Resources

- *Hit the Road* is an interactive personal finance game that teaches young people the value of saving, budgeting, and making smart financial decisions while on a road trip across the country.

- "Your Financial Future is Brighter with Savings" video featuring NCUA Board Chairman Debbie Matz highlights the importance of saving.

- A variety of videos, webinars and blog posts highlight the importance of consumer financial protection and how consumers can protect themselves from fraud, scams, and other risky financial behavior.

Actions to Preserve Minority Depository Institutions

NCUA undertook several initiatives designed to preserve minority depository institutions during the reporting period. Considering that 92 percent of the minority depository institutions are classified as either low-income or small (with assets of $50 million or less), NCUA's support to minority depository institutions is primarily provided through programs administered by the Office of Small Credit Union Initiatives. Additionally, NCUA's regional offices and the Office of Consumer Protection play essential roles in preserving minority depository institutions.

The Minority Depository Institution Preservation Program offers a variety of initiatives to preserve and strengthen minority depository institutions. The program features are designed to help minority depository institutions thrive, and they will vary depending on the particular needs of the minority depository institution. While the policy statement is being finalized, NCUA has taken steps to preserve minority depository institutions and formalize systems to document these efforts and monitor our progress. While additional work is needed to fully develop these systems, the initial system dataset, from July 1, 2013, through June 30, 2014, revealed notable actions taken by the agency's staff to preserve minority depository institutions.

Preserving the Number of Minority Depository Institutions

NCUA implemented many initiatives to preserve minority depository institutions as illustrated throughout this report. These efforts consisted of various forms of training, technical assistance and educational programs. Self-certification as a minority depository institution and participation in the Minority Depository Institution Preservation Program are voluntary. The agency allows minority depository institutions to change their minority designation and drop in and out of the program at any time, which results in fluctuating numbers.

Additionally, while it appears that the total number of minority depository credit unions declined in the reporting period, in actuality, the reduction can be attributed to NCUA clarifying the eligibility criteria. As of June 30, 2013, a total of 805 credit unions self-certified as meeting the minority depository definition. Many of these credit unions initially self-certified as minority institutions based solely on their membership statistics. However, based on the proposed minority depository institution definition that considers a majority of minority members and senior management officials, minority depository institutions totaled 688 as of June 30, 2014. While 129 credit unions decertified as a result of the clarification, 12 additional credit unions certified during the reporting period.

Preserving the Character of Minority Depository Institutions

Whenever possible, NCUA's regional staff seeks to preserve the character of troubled minority depository institutions by encouraging a merger into another minority depository institution.[3] However, in the cases of voluntary mergers or voluntary liquidations, NCUA has little control over a board of directors' selection of a financially sound merger partner or decision to liquidate the institution. During the reporting period, a total of 30 minority depository institutions either merged with another institution or were liquidated. The chart shows the percentage of mergers and liquidations involving minority depository institutions over the reporting period.

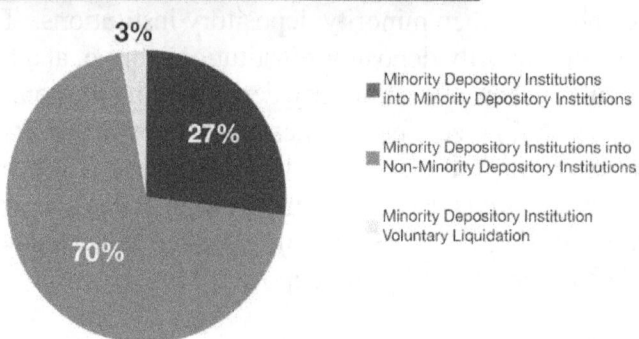

Of the 30 minority depository institutions, 28 institutions, or 93 percent, were mergers, while the remaining two institutions, or 7 percent, involved liquidations. One minority depository institution was involuntarily liquidated as a precursor to a purchase and assumption by a non-minority depository institution. One voluntary liquidation of a minority depository institution was approved by the credit union's board of directors as a pay-out to members.

Of the 29 consolidations, NCUA was successful in merging eight institutions, or 27 percent, into another minority depository institution to preserve their minority character. Twenty-one institutions, or 70 percent of the 30 minority depository institutions, were either merged with or assumed by non-minority depository institutions. Of the 21 mergers or assumptions into non-minority institutions, 15 were voluntary. Six mergers, characterized as non-voluntary, did go forward despite NCUA's attempts to locate other interested minority credit unions.

---

[3] NCUA Rules and Regulations, Section 701.14(b)(3) defines "troubled condition" as any insured natural person credit union that has been assigned a CAMEL composite rating of 4 or 5 by NCUA or the state supervisor, or that has been granted assistance as outlined under Section 208 or 216 of the Federal Credit Union Act.

Providing Technical Assistance to Prevent Insolvency of Minority Depository Institutions

NCUA provides many forms of technical assistance to prevent the insolvency of minority depository institutions. Examples of NCUA's assistance during the reporting period include:

- An examiner worked with management to locate a new sponsor willing to provide sufficient financial support to the minority depository institution. The new sponsor donated capital, agreed to pay operating expenses, and housed the institution.

- Examiners provided extensive guidance to three newly chartered minority depository institutions—with frequent onsite contacts, phone calls and emails— to help management develop sound policies and procedures, and understand potential risks and the need for internal controls.

- Examiners and economic development specialists assisted six minority depository institutions in developing and getting approval for Net Worth Restoration Plans to help build capital, sustain operations and improve the financial health of these six credit unions.

- An examiner worked with new management on strategic issues, including applying for a Community Development Financial Institution certification to obtain grant funds and secondary capital from the U.S. Treasury.

- An examiner facilitated another credit union providing staff to temporarily replace the manager of a faltering minority depository institution. This action allowed for continued operations and member service while the sponsor searched for a permanent manager.

- An examiner facilitated a request for continuation after the financial support from a sponsor expired. This allowed the minority institution time to restructure its operations and become a stand-alone institution.

- Economic development specialists provided guidance on using secondary capital to replace non-member deposits, and provided information on potential sources of secondary capital.

NCUA staff will continue to monitor the effectiveness of these efforts. NCUA will also explore additional and unique ways of providing this assistance to minority depository institutions to help them sustain their operations and thrive.

Promoting the Creation of Minority Depository Institutions

NCUA promotes the creation of new minority depository institutions by providing interested groups with assistance in preparing the new charter and field of membership applications. The goals of the chartering and field of membership policies are to:

- Encourage the formation of credit unions;
- Uphold the provisions of the Federal Credit Union Act;
- Promote thrift and credit extension;
- Promote credit union safety and soundness; and
- Make quality credit union service available to all eligible persons.

NCUA's Office of Consumer Protection processes charter and field of membership applications. Additionally, NCUA's economic development specialists provide:

- Groups with assistance in developing charter applications and acceptable business plans; and
- Credit unions with assistance in developing field of membership expansions, including adding an occupational or associational group, adding an underserved area, and converting charters to another common bond.

During the reporting period, NCUA approved one new charter to a Native American institution. The new charter was issued to Northern Eagle Federal Credit Union in October 2013. This credit union serves employees of the Bois Fort Band of Chippewa and other related select occupational groups.

Also, Maui Federal Credit Union, an Asian American institution, was approved for a community charter conversion in August 2013. The conversion allowed the credit union to serve persons who live, work, worship, or attend school in, and businesses and other legal entities located on the island of Maui, Hawaii.

Providing Training, Technical Assistance, and Educational Programs

NCUA's training, technical assistance and educational programs are predominantly provided by the Office of Small Credit Union Initiatives. Examiners also play a vital role in providing training and guidance to minority depository institutions under their supervision.

From July 1, 2013, to June 30, 2014, the training, technical assistance and educational programs provided to minority depository institutions included consulting services, low-income designation approvals, grants and loans, and other training and education programs as discussed below.

Consulting and Guidance

NCUA provides consulting services to officials of newly chartered, small, minority and low-income designated credit unions for a variety of operational and management matters. Also, examiners work with credit union management to resolve any concerns that arose during an examination.

From July 1, 2013, to June 30, 2014, economic development specialists in conjunction with examiners provided guidance on 215 areas of interest for 148 minority depository institutions. The chart below depicts the various types of consulting and guidance provided by NCUA.

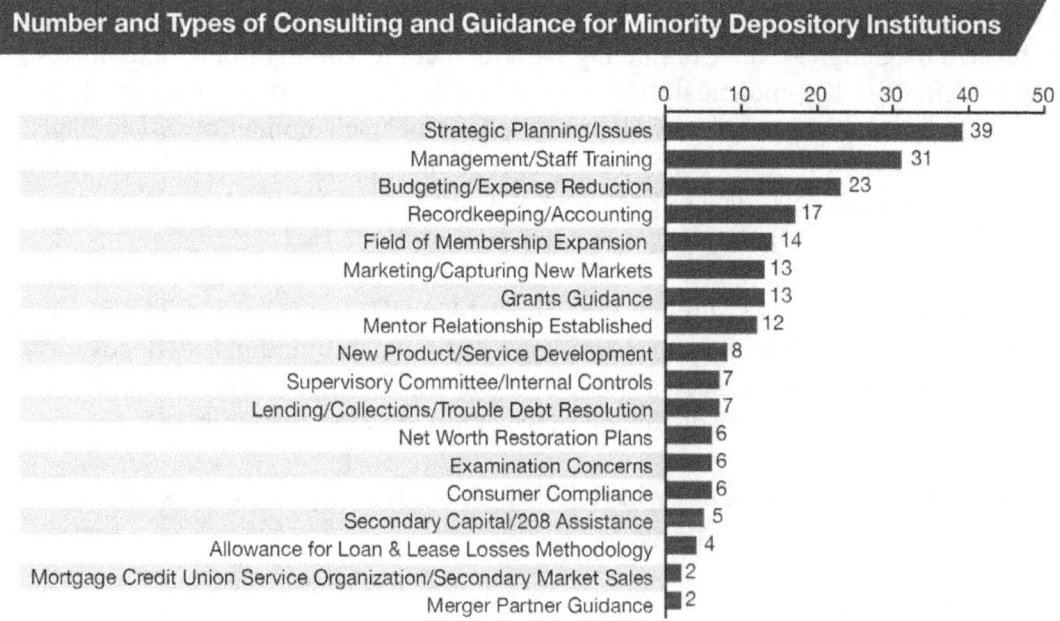

The most common consulting and guidance provided to the minority depository institutions involved strategic planning and issues, management and staff training, budgeting and expense reduction, recordkeeping and accounting, field of membership expansion guidance, grant guidance, and marketing to and capturing new markets.

Low-Income Designations

NCUA's Office of Consumer Protection designated 20 minority depository institutions as low-income during the reporting period (see Appendix 2).

To qualify as a low-income credit union, a majority of a credit union's members must meet low-income thresholds based on data from the 2010 United States Census.[4] The designation offers several benefits to credit unions, including grants and loans from NCUA's Community Development Revolving Loan Fund, access to secondary capital and greater member business lending opportunities.

As of June 30, 2014, a total of 466 minority depository institutions were designated as low-income, which represents 68 percent of all minority depository institutions. The 466 minority depository institutions also represents 22 percent of all (2,074) credit unions designated as low-income.

Grants and Loans

Established by Congress, the Community Development Revolving Loan Fund makes loans and grants to low-income designated credit unions only. Congress established this fund to stimulate economic development in low-income communities. The funds for grants and loans primarily come from congressional appropriations and loan interest and principal repayments. The Office of Small Credit Union Initiatives administers the program.

Grants: From July 1, 2013, through June 30, 2014, NCUA awarded $21,742 in grants from the Community Development Revolving Loan Fund to four minority depository institutions for urgent needs, such as building repairs and equipment replacement following a natural disaster or disruption in the credit union's operations.

In addition, 67 minority depository institutions received other grant awards totaling $376,168 for the following purposes:

- Financial Capability,
- New Products and Services,
- Staff and Officials Training,
- Student Internships, and
- Community Development Financial Institution Certification Assistance.

Grants to minority depository institutions totaled $397,910 or 28 percent of $1,423,711 in grant funding awarded during the reporting period. Appendix 3 contains a list of the minority depository institutions that received these grants.

---

4 "Low-income members" are members with a family income 80 percent or less than the median family income for the metropolitan area where they live or national metropolitan area, whichever is greater. Members enrolled as students in a college, university, high school, or vocational school also qualify as low income members. See NCUA Rules and Regulation, Section 701.34, for the full definition.

Loans: During the same reporting period, three minority depository institutions received $1,150,000, or 26 percent, of the $4,400,000 in total loans disbursed. Most loan proceeds were used for the purposes of providing vehicle and consumer loans and alternatives to payday lending. Appendix 3 also contains a complete list of the minority depository institutions that received loans from NCUA.

Training and Educational Programs

NCUA continues to offer training, through the Office of Small Credit Union Initiatives, to credit unions, regardless of asset size, in various forms, including workshops, videos, webinars, and newsletters. All training is provided at no cost to credit unions.

Workshops and Boot Camps: NCUA-sponsored workshops and leadership development boot camps were held in cities throughout the U.S., including Honolulu, Birmingham, Independence, Dallas, Buffalo, Memphis, Columbus, New Orleans, San Antonio, Pittsburgh, Baton Rouge, Los Angeles, Chicago and Minneapolis.

During the reporting period, 378 attendees from 221 minority depository institutions participated in NCUA's workshops and boot camps. The attendees from minority institutions represented 33 percent of the officials and staff that attended the workshops and leadership development boot camps.

During these training sessions, leading experts and NCUA staff shared their insight and guidance on the following topics:

- Bank Secrecy Act and Money Service Business
- Marketing in the Digital Age
- Protecting Your Credit Union from the Rising Trend of Employment Practice Lawsuits
- Marketing Advertising
- Examination Modernization
- Hidden in Plain Sight — Dishonest Employees
- Electronic Services
- Bank Secrecy Act
- Understanding the Financial Statements
- Regulatory Compliance
- Understanding the Key Ratios for Board Members
- Succession Planning
- Fair Lending
- Strategic Planning
- Improving Internal Controls

Also, in late 2013, workshop attendees in a few locations participated in a special poverty simulation presented by the National Credit Union Foundation. The poverty simulation was an exercise providing participants the opportunity, and challenge, of walking in the shoes of a low-income individual. The simulation was designed to increase awareness of how credit unions can make a difference in the lives of low-income members and young adults beginning their financial lives.

Videos and Webinars: The agency developed videos and webinars to provide training to educate credit union officials and staff on a variety of topics that are helpful to minority depository institutions. NCUA offers this training on the agency's website and its YouTube channel. Some of the topics featured include:

- Financial Literacy: Putting Your Mission into Action
- Bank Secrecy Act, Office of Foreign Asset Control and FinCEN Compliance
- Small-Dollar Lending
- Member Business Lending
- Field of Membership Expansions
- Profiling Products and Services for Underserved Members
- Business Continuity Planning and Disaster Recovery
- Succession Planning
- Fraud Prevention Series
- Credit Union Collaborations
- Mobile Applications — Mobile Banking and Remote Deposits
- NCUA Consumer Protection Updates
- Using NCUA's Credit Union Online Profile System

Publications: The Office of Small Credit Union Initiatives prepared several publications and white papers as additional forms of education to low-income, minority, and small credit unions. Found on NCUA's website, examples of the agency's recent publications include:

- Marketing Tips, Technology and Tools for Credit Unions with Limited Resources
- Truth in Mergers: A Guide for Merging Credit Unions
- Credit Union Leadership Resource Manual

Outreach and Partnerships Programs: NCUA continued to focus on improving the agency's communications and education with low-income, minority and small credit unions through a monthly newsletter, an online Frequently Asked Question (FAQ+) system and partnerships.

FOCUS is a monthly electronic newsletter providing news, educational articles, and upcoming opportunities relating to consulting services, grant and loan rounds, webinars, videos, and other training to help low-income, minority and small credit unions achieve success. The *FOCUS* e-newsletter is available online at http://go.usa.gov/WxhT.

FAQ+ is an online search engine that provides answers to common questions credit union managers and officials ask about training opportunities, grants and other subjects. It improves service to small, minority, low-income and new credit unions by helping them become better informed and being readily accessible. Available on the Office of Small Credit Union Initiatives' microsite, FAQ+ provides access to other resources for credit union officials such as supervisory guidance, white papers, videos, agency forms and other content.

Collaborating with government agencies, industry leaders and other nonprofits is another effective way NCUA achieves its goals for sustaining small and minority credit union operations. The Office of Small Credit Union Initiatives partners with these types of organizations as a way to expand credit union access to resources beyond those provided by NCUA. The chart below includes examples of these partnerships.

Partners	Description
Assets for Independence	Federal individual development account program
AssetPlatform.org	Online resources for non-profit financial services professionals
Community Development Financial Institutions Program	Financial and technical assistance programs to benefit economically distressed and underserved communities
Office of Foreign Assets Control	Technical assistance and guidance regarding OFAC compliance
Net Impact	Online service to help engage qualified staff volunteers
SCORE	A variety of free and inexpensive business resources, including mentoring, counseling, and training

This chart references material created and maintained by organizations other than NCUA. NCUA cannot endorse or guarantee the accuracy, completeness, or timeliness of information provided by third parties. Each credit union is responsible for ensuring that any program it implements is appropriate for its institution and complies with the laws of its jurisdiction.

In addition, the agency performed outreach to minority credit unions and trade associations serving minority depository institutions during the reporting year. These trade associations included the National Federation of Community Development Credit Unions, the African American Credit Union Coalition and the National Latino Credit Unions and Professionals. NCUA attended, exhibited and gave speeches at their annual conferences. The agency also held meetings with these organizations to obtain their input on issues affecting the minority credit union community, such as the proposed minority depository institution definition and the proposed Minority Depository Institution Preservation Program.

NCUA continues to view its role as encouraging and enabling federally insured credit unions to serve all of their members, including minority and low- and moderate-income individuals and groups. Collaborations with the minority credit union community will help NCUA better understand their challenges and provide potential solutions for sustaining minority depository institutions.

Conclusion

NCUA is dedicated to preserving minority depository institutions, encouraging new institutions and developing programs designed not just to sustain minority depository institutions, but to help them thrive. This second annual report on minority depository institution covers the period from July 1, 2013, through June 30, 2014, and provides detailed data pertaining to the structure and financial condition of minority depository institutions under NCUA's regulatory authority, as well as programs undertaken by NCUA's regional offices, Office of Small Credit Union Initiatives and Office of Consumer Protection to preserve and encourage these institutions.

As of June 30, 2014, a total of 688 credit unions self-certified as meeting the minority criteria, representing nearly 11 percent of all federally insured credit unions. The states with the highest concentration of minority depository institutions are Texas, California, New York, Hawaii and Louisiana.

According to June 30, 2014, Call Report data, minority depository institutions have aggregate total assets of $36.9 billion and are owned by 4.5 million members. Excluding Multi-Cultural institutions, the Hispanic American and Asian American institutions comprise the largest portion of minority depository institutions' share deposits based on their average asset size. Their average total assets are approximately $84 million for Hispanic American institutions and $81 million for Asian American institutions.

The vast majority of minority depository institutions are financially sound with an overall CAMEL composite rating of 3 or better. Ninety-nine percent of these institutions are either well or adequately capitalized. Sixty-five percent of these institutions are earning sufficient revenue to cover their operating costs, while the remaining 35 percent are experiencing challenges and may need monetary assistance to adequately meet the financial needs of their membership. Sixty-one percent have loan delinquency rates in excess of 1 percent, demonstrating the need for additional financial literacy education among their members.

NCUA's Minority Depository Institution Preservation Program is still in its early stages of development. This report highlights NCUA's efforts under this program which include:

- Issuing a new credit union charter to a minority depository institution.
- Expanding another minority depository institution's field of membership through a community charter conversion.

- Approving low-income designations to minority depository institutions to provide access to monetary assistance, such as grants, loans, non-member deposits and secondary capital.
- Providing officials and staff of minority depository institutions with training and education through consulting services, workshops, leadership development boot camps, webinars, videos, publications, newsletters, online search engines and partnerships.
- Encouraging the merger of a troubled minority depository institution into another minority depository institution whenever possible.

NCUA will continue its work through the Office of Minority and Women Inclusion and other offices toward preserving and encouraging minority depository institutions, as well as developing and refining systems to track these efforts. Looking to the future, NCUA will continue to build new partnerships and collaborate with organizations predominantly serving minority depository institutions. Staff will also explore ways to solicit input from minority depository institutions on how to best serve their needs. Finally, NCUA will work with other supervisory and regulatory agencies to collaborate and share best practices for serving minority depository institutions.

Appendix 1: Minority Depository Institutions by State

ALABAMA MINORITY DEPOSITORY INSTITUTIONS

CHARTER	NAME	CITY	STATE	ASSETS	MINORITY TYPE	MEMBERS	LOW INCOME
12837	MARVEL CITY	Bessemer	AL	$7,446,678	Black American	980	Yes
1610	PEOPLE'S FIRST	Birmingham	AL	$6,099,628	Black American	1,015	Yes
15938	SIXTH AVENUE BAPTIST	Birmingham	AL	$4,529,857	Black American	907	Yes
16858	NEW PILGRIM	Birmingham	AL	$1,581,910	Black American	834	Yes
24583	NRS COMMUNITY DEVELOPMENT	Birmingham	AL	$950,974	Black American	361	Yes
62356	L&N EMPLOYEES	Birmingham	AL	$9,710,301	Asian American, Black American	1,300	No
62599	FEDERAL EMPLOYEES	Birmingham	AL	$14,312,674	Asian American, Black American, Hispanic American	1,463	No
64232	1ST RESOURCE	Birmingham	AL	$28,968,604	Black American	2,698	No
64594	FIREMAN'S	Birmingham	AL	$4,593,834	Black American	830	No
64603	ALABAMA LAW ENFORCEMENT CREDIT UNION	Birmingham	AL	$8,007,145	Black American	1,580	No
17311	DEMOPOLIS	Demopolis	AL	$674,495	Asian American, Hispanic American, Native American	827	Yes
22131	FOGCE	Eutaw	AL	$1,293,389	Black American	652	Yes
13018	CLARKE EDUCATORS	Grove Hill	AL	$3,594,208	Black American	770	Yes
11422	PROGRESSIVE	Mobile	AL	$5,706,812	Black American	880	Yes
64725	SHORELINE	Mobile	AL	$8,800,102	Black American	2,881	No
14314	TRI-RIVERS	Montgomery	AL	$17,679,428	Black American	7,144	Yes
64598	ALABAMA STATE EMPLOYEES	Montgomery	AL	$220,210,650	Black American	27,997	No
9554	COUNCILL	Normal	AL	$3,338,394	Black American	816	Yes
23893	EVONIK EMPLOYEES	Theodore	AL	$7,112,732	Black American	847	Yes
64464	TUSCALOOSA COUNTY	Tuscaloosa	AL	$6,979,650	Black American	1,448	No
2791	TUSKEGEE	Tuskegee	AL	$6,097,374	Asian American, Black American, Hispanic American, Native American	3,725	Yes
6311	TVH	Tuskegee	AL	$4,323,724	Black American	748	Yes
Total No. of Minority Depository Institutions for Alabama: 22				**$372,012,563**		**60,703**	

ARIZONA MINORITY DEPOSITORY INSTITUTIONS

CHARTER	NAME	CITY	STATE	ASSETS	MINORITY TYPE	MEMBERS	LOW INCOME
61451	JACL	Glendale	AZ	$795,897	Asian American	186	No

CHARTER	NAME	CITY	STATE	ASSETS	MINORITY TYPE	MEMBERS	LOW INCOME
4915	A. E. A.	Yuma	AZ	$241,351,399	Hispanic American	39,863	Yes

Total No. of Minority Depository Institutions for Arizona: 2 — **$242,147,296** — **40,049**

ARKANSAS MINORITY DEPOSITORY INSTITUTIONS

CHARTER	NAME	CITY	STATE	ASSETS	MINORITY TYPE	MEMBERS	LOW INCOME
24435	U.P. EMPLOYEES	North Little RO	AR	$4,555,122	Black American	1,290	Yes
7700	ARKANSAS AM & N COLLEGE	Pine Bluff	AR	$2,339,977	Black American	972	Yes
24423	PINE BLUFF POSTAL	Pine Bluff	AR	$854,275	Black American	143	Yes

Total No. of Minority Depository Institutions for Arkansas: 3 — **$7,749,374** — **2,405**

CALIFORNIA MINORITY DEPOSITORY INSTITUTIONS

CHARTER	NAME	CITY	STATE	ASSETS	MINORITY TYPE	MEMBERS	LOW INCOME
61125	FINANCIAL BENEFITS	Alameda	CA	$19,241,934	Asian American, Black American, Hispanic American	2,755	No
20111	UNITED AMERICA WEST	Arleta	CA	$4,260,524	Hispanic American	553	Yes
4900	COOPERATIVE CENTER	Berkeley	CA	$106,869,558	Asian American, Black American, Hispanic American, Native American	12,728	Yes
8230	TECHNICOLOR	Burbank	CA	$41,605,411	Asian American, Hispanic American	4,469	No
21872	AUTO CLUB	Cerritos	CA	$27,797,848	Hispanic American	4,826	No
19266	COLTON	Colton	CA	$6,425,892	Hispanic American	1,160	Yes
4475	COMPTON MUNICIPAL EMPLOYEES	Compton	CA	$920,118	Black American	546	Yes
68356	FIRST IMPERIAL	El Centro	CA	$77,150,805	Hispanic American	14,930	No
9004	SO VAL TEL	Fresno	CA	$15,462,735	Asian American, Black American, Hispanic American, Native American	1,996	No
24552	FRESNO COUNTY	Fresno	CA	$540,630,430	Asian American, Black American, Hispanic American	61,364	Yes
65059	NIKKEI	Gardena	CA	$68,811,096	Asian American	5,452	No
1207	LOS ANGELES	Glendale	CA	$794,859,420	Asian American, Black American, Hispanic American	52,715	No
7557	GLENDALE	Glendale	CA	$61,985,228	Asian American, Black American, Hispanic American, Native American	4,321	No
6135	DAIJO	Los Angeles	CA	$2,476,775	Asian American	309	No
9255	WESTERN STATES REGIONAL	Los Angeles	CA	$693,094	Hispanic American	374	Yes

10648	MARYKNOLL OF LA	Los Angeles	CA	$964,343	Asian American	165	No
10767	PEOPLES IND CHURCH	Los Angeles	CA	$74,447	Black American	121	Yes
16570	LOS ANGELES LEE	Los Angeles	CA	$595,385	Asian American	119	Yes
19640	ZION HILL BAPTIST CHURCH	Los Angeles	CA	$206,951	Black American	149	Yes
22965	GUIDANCE CHURCH OF RELIGIOUS SCIENCE	Los Angeles	CA	$121,009	Black American	114	Yes
24506	EPISCOPAL COMMUNITY	Los Angeles	CA	$5,049,237	Black American, Hispanic American	2,340	Yes
24549	HANIN	Los Angeles	CA	$24,275,893	Asian American	3,090	Yes
62092	MUSICIANS' INTERGUILD	Los Angeles	CA	$75,069,715	Asian American, Black American	6,666	No
63589	JACOM	Los Angeles	CA	$80,694,659	Asian American	9,737	No
68459	USC	Los Angeles	CA	$391,784,616	Asian American, Black American, Hispanic American	57,914	Yes
68503	FIRST CITY	Los Angeles	CA	$525,351,748	Hispanic American	54,981	No
9119	MERCED SCHOOL EMPLOYEES	Merced	CA	$407,666,597	Asian American, Hispanic American	35,539	No
4633	CAMINO	Montebello	CA	$130,748,826	Hispanic American	12,410	Yes
65674	BAKERY EMPLOYEES	Montebello	CA	$7,034,413	Hispanic American	1,360	No
15784	C R C	Norco	CA	$8,503,157	Hispanic American	1,901	No
21263	TAYLOR MEMORIAL UNITED METHODIST	Oakland	CA	$27,592	Black American	107	Yes
22015	ILWU - FSC	Oakland	CA	$23,249,031	Black American, Hispanic American	2,889	Yes
24687	FAITH BASED	Oceanside	CA	$1,131,953	Black American, Hispanic American	471	Yes
14542	ONTARIO MONTCLAIR SCHOOLS	Ontario	CA	$88,439,205	Hispanic American	7,074	No
21532	U.P.S. EMPLOYEES	Ontario	CA	$30,502,296	Hispanic American	5,782	No
24736	PACOIMA DEVELOPMENT	Pacoima	CA	$4,148,241	Hispanic American	1,014	Yes
66703	WESCOM CENTRAL	Pasadena	CA	$2,767,361,030	Asian American, Black American, Hispanic American, Native American	192,533	No
14739	CAL POLY	Pomona	CA	$11,953,284	Asian American, Black American, Hispanic American, Native American	2,403	Yes
3526	SCHOOLS	Rancho Dominguez	CA	$111,251,127	Asian American, Black American, Hispanic American, Native American	16,906	Yes
11194	STAR HARBOR	Rancho Dominguez	CA	$14,237,229	Hispanic American	3,046	Yes
63630	ATCHISON VILLAGE	Richmond	CA	$8,206,699	Hispanic American	1,260	Yes

65113	ALLUS CREDIT UNION	Salinas	CA	$34,804,418	Hispanic American	3,751	No
68027	1ST VALLEY	San Bernardino	CA	$34,005,252	Asian American, Black American, Hispanic American, Native American	3,510	Yes
68463	NORTH COUNTY	San Diego	CA	$58,781,259	Asian American, Black American, Hispanic American, Native American	3,763	No
20720	L. A. MISSION	San Fernando	CA	$6,561,236	Hispanic American	1,574	Yes
21417	CALVARY BAPTIST OF PACOIMA	San Fernando	CA	$150,132	Black American	304	Yes
7826	S F MUNICIPAL RAILWAY EMP	San Francisco	CA	$6,115,597	Black American, Hispanic American	785	No
16547	SAN FRANCISCO LEE	San Francisco	CA	$11,608,899	Asian American	1,048	No
19554	BETHEL A.M.E. SAN FRANCISCO	San Francisco	CA	$417,713	Black American	322	No
23780	NORTHEAST COMMUNITY	San Francisco	CA	$10,524,828	Asian American	1,472	Yes
64892	JONES METHODIST CHURCH	San Francisco	CA	$541,860	Black American	313	No
24391	CHERRY EMPLOYEES	Santa Ana	CA	$3,960,822	Hispanic American	517	No
24520	SANTA ANA	Santa Ana	CA	$62,539,005	Asian American, Black American, Hispanic American, Native American	6,472	No
24776	COMUNIDAD LATINA	Santa Ana	CA	$3,969,630	Hispanic American	2,173	Yes
64029	SANTA CRUZ COMMUNITY	Santa Cruz	CA	$108,059,447	Hispanic American	11,600	Yes
17841	LIMONEIRA	Santa Paula	CA	$4,933,341	Hispanic American	686	Yes
13254	CORRECTIONS	Soledad	CA	$13,025,365	Asian American, Black American, Hispanic American, Native American	2,685	Yes
60024	PRIORITY ONE	South Pasadena	CA	$148,358,491	Black American, Hispanic American	25,285	No
64576	SAN FERNANDO VALLEY JAPANESE	Sylmar	CA	$1,036,530	Asian American	289	No
64122	VALLEY OAK	Three Rivers	CA	$46,797,034	Hispanic American	6,726	Yes
18623	CALCOM	Torrance	CA	$63,447,583	Asian American, Hispanic American	8,228	No
4393	SUNKIST EMPLOYEES	Valencia	CA	$5,862,788	Hispanic American	872	Yes
11943	KAIPERM NORTH BAY	Vallejo	CA	$34,171,727	Asian American, Black American	4,315	No
12029	UNITED CATHOLICS	West Covina	CA	$29,374,138	Hispanic American	3,625	No
17652	CEDARS-SINAI	West Hollywood	CA	$22,095,881	Asian American, Black American, Hispanic American	4,049	No
64382	UNITED FINANCIAL	Whittier	CA	$37,118,522	Hispanic American	2,596	No
24052	FAMILY	Wilmington	CA	$7,452,515	Hispanic American	1,640	Yes

| 68053 | SIERRA CENTRAL | Yuba City | CA | $730,823,622 | Asian American, Black American, Hispanic American | 60,987 | No |

| Total No. of Minority Depository Institutions for California: 68 | | | | $7,974,377,186 | | 748,176 | |

COLORADO MINORITY DEPOSITORY INSTITUTIONS

CHARTER	NAME	CITY	STATE	ASSETS	MINORITY TYPE	MEMBERS	LOW INCOME
63468	VALLEY EDUCATORS	Alamosa	CO	$4,690,997	Hispanic American	1,082	Yes
65471	GUADALUPE PARISH	Antonito	CO	$20,609,694	Hispanic American	2,943	Yes
12056	HARRISON DISTRICT NO 2	Colorado Spring	CO	$11,897,387	Asian American, Black American, Hispanic American	1,661	Yes
65726	WEST DENVER COMMUNITY	Denver	CO	$9,115,585	Hispanic American	1,873	Yes
1479	ARKANSAS VALLEY	Las Animas	CO	$11,431,238	Hispanic American	3,002	Yes
1499	PUEBLO GOVERNMENT AGENCIES	Pueblo	CO	$27,201,063	Hispanic American	3,642	Yes
2449	PUEBLO HORIZONS	Pueblo	CO	$27,532,791	Hispanic American	3,610	Yes

| Total No. of Minority Depository Institutions for Colorado: 7 | | | | $112,478,755 | | 17,813 | |

CONNECTICUT MINORITY DEPOSITORY INSTITUTIONS

CHARTER	NAME	CITY	STATE	ASSETS	MINORITY TYPE	MEMBERS	LOW INCOME
23896	EAST END BAPTIST TABERNACLE	Bridgeport	CT	$186,552	Black American	399	Yes
24723	FAIRFIELD COUNTY	Fairfield	CT	$30,548,074	Black American, Hispanic American	4,327	Yes
1863	CONNECTICUT TRANSIT	Hartford	CT	$1,102,897	Black American, Hispanic American	613	Yes
6733	HARTFORD MUNICIPAL EMPLOYEES	Hartford	CT	$42,973,313	Black American, Hispanic American	7,095	Yes
19	NEW HAVEN TEACHERS	New Haven	CT	$9,782,948	Black American, Hispanic American	1,489	No
1153	SARGENT & COMPANY EMPLOYEES	New Haven	CT	$3,521,762	Asian American, Black American, Hispanic American, Native American	675	No
23835	IMMANUEL BAPTIST CHURCH	New Haven	CT	$118,579	Black American	188	Yes
23411	CONNECTICUT	North Haven	CT	$7,177,069	Black American, Hispanic American	2,097	No
10845	FAITH TABERNACLE BAPTIST	Stamford	CT	$197,100	Black American	271	Yes
21614	FIRST BAPTIST CHURCH (STRATFORD)	Stratford	CT	$265,443	Black American	300	No

| Total No. of Minority Depository Institutions for Connecticut: 10 | | | | $95,873,737 | | 17,454 | |

DELAWARE MINORITY DEPOSITORY INSTITUTIONS

CHARTER	NAME	CITY	STATE	ASSETS	MINORITY TYPE	MEMBERS	LOW INCOME
19170	MILFORD MEMORIAL	Milford	DE	$3,199,232	Asian American, Black American, Hispanic American, Native American	935	No
15426	AMERICAN SPIRIT	Newark	DE	$65,460,833	Black American	12,305	No
24845	STEPPING STONES COMMUNITY	Wilmington	DE	$1,419,315	Black American	250	Yes

| Total No. of Minority Depository Institutions for Delaware: 3 | | | | $70,079,380 | | 13,490 | |

DISTRICT OF COLOMBIA MINORITY DEPOSITORY INSTITUTIONS

CHARTER	NAME	CITY	STATE	ASSETS	MINORITY TYPE	MEMBERS	LOW INCOME
266	LIBRARY OF CONGRESS	Washington	DC	$223,688,850	Black American	9,484	No
367	PEPCO	Washington	DC	$33,273,028	Black American	2,602	No
538	GOVERNMENT PRINTING OFFICE	Washington	DC	$37,304,549	Black American	3,649	Yes
648	HOWARD UNIVERSITY EMPLOYEES	Washington	DC	$11,326,519	Black American	2,066	Yes
1821	DISTRICT OF COLUMBIA TEACHERS	Washington	DC	$44,381,348	Black American	6,289	Yes
2942	NLRB	Washington	DC	$19,288,391	Black American	3,062	No
3764	TRANSIT EMPLOYEES	Washington	DC	$97,870,706	Black American	17,083	Yes
4037	HUD	Washington	DC	$50,329,442	Black American	5,599	No
5227	ASBURY	Washington	DC	$391,394	Black American	208	Yes
6088	D C FIRE DEPARTMENT	Washington	DC	$6,776,622	Black American	1,557	No
6464	PAHO/WHO	Washington	DC	$202,169,662	Hispanic American	4,986	No
6506	MT GILEAD	Washington	DC	$50,456	Black American	62	Yes
9613	SARGENT	Washington	DC	$327,609	Black American	407	No
14176	IDB-IIC	Washington	DC	$481,296,292	Hispanic American	9,826	No
15174	LEE	Washington	DC	$11,068,636	Asian American	625	No
16046	HOYA	Washington	DC	$20,272,501	Black American, Hispanic American	4,102	Yes
16411	DC	Washington	DC	$52,816,530	Black American	10,316	Yes
17874	ST. GABRIELS	Washington	DC	$408,450	Black American	158	No
20377	PEOPLES-NEIGHBORHOOD	Washington	DC	$202,139	Black American	254	Yes
22323	JOHN WESLEY AME ZION CHURCH	Washington	DC	$86,598	Black American	173	No
22686	NAPFE	Washington	DC	$3,796,928	Black American	1,564	No
24073	PARAMOUNT BAPTIST CHURCH	Washington	DC	$101,413	Black American	505	No
24219	MT. AIRY BAPTIST CHURCH	Washington	DC	$1,378,709	Black American	509	Yes
24262	PHI BETA SIGMA	Washington	DC	$428,799	Black American, Native American	1,695	No
Total No. of Minority Depository Institutions for the District of Columbia: 24				**$1,299,035,571**		**86,781**	

FLORIDA MINORITY DEPOSITORY INSTITUTIONS

CHARTER	NAME	CITY	STATE	ASSETS	MINORITY TYPE	MEMBERS	LOW INCOME
23948	COMMUNITY TRUST	Apopka	FL	$7,614,973	Hispanic American	2,587	Yes
11746	BROWARD HEALTHCARE	Fort Lauderdale	FL	$61,816,794	Black American, Hispanic American	9,277	No
2654	DUCOTE	Jacksonville	FL	$3,164,454	Black American	1,190	Yes
67630	MADISON EDUCATION ASSOC.	Madison	FL	$4,306,307	Black American	765	No

1068	COMPASS FINANCIAL	Medley	FL	$22,934,899	Black American, Hispanic American	2,759	Yes
11791	ST. JAMES A M E CHURCH	Miami	FL	$449,983	Black American	544	Yes
14391	BAPTIST HEALTH SOUTH FLORIDA	Miami	FL	$49,353,466	Black American, Hispanic American	11,065	Yes
23041	SOUTH FLORIDA	Miami	FL	$34,305,510	Black American, Hispanic American	3,980	Yes
67338	ELECTRICIANS' LOCAL 349	Miami	FL	$4,148,377	Black American, Hispanic American	768	No
24593	NORTH DADE COMMUNITY DEVELOPMENT	Miami Gardens	FL	$4,022,035	Black American	652	Yes
24718	JETSTREAM	Miami Lakes	FL	$163,243,199	Hispanic American	20,126	Yes
68476	TROPICAL FINANCIAL	Miramar	FL	$555,283,653	Black American, Hispanic American	54,408	No
67341	JEFFERSON COUNTY TEACHERS	Monticello	FL	$7,934,142	Black American	1,040	No
67318	POMPANO BEACH CITY EMP.	Pompano Beach	FL	$16,952,140	Black American	1,624	No
187	FLORIDA A & M UNIVERSITY	Tallahassee	FL	$19,881,855	Black American	3,323	Yes
22380	FCAMEC	Tallahassee	FL	$1,800,340	Black American	553	Yes
22196	TAMPA LONGSHOREMEN'S	Tampa	FL	$478,342	Black American	278	Yes
16834	TOWN OF PALM BEACH	West Palm Beach	FL	$2,750,935	Black American	383	Yes
Total No. of Minority Depository Institutions for Florida: 18				**$960,441,404**		**115,322**	

GEORGIA MINORITY DEPOSITORY INSTITUTIONS

CHARTER	NAME	CITY	STATE	ASSETS	MINORITY TYPE	MEMBERS	LOW INCOME
24161	SPC	Atlanta	GA	$1,151,858	Black American	1,363	No
24546	BIG BETHEL A.M.E. CHURCH	Atlanta	GA	$345,124	Black American	306	Yes
67383	CREDIT UNION OF ATLANTA	Atlanta	GA	$73,390,830	Black American	19,137	No
67505	1ST CHOICE	Atlanta	GA	$21,499,046	Black American	9,156	Yes
67706	FORT MCPHERSON	Atlanta	GA	$21,630,318	Black American	5,395	No
14103	TABERNACLE	Augusta	GA	$164,317	Black American	394	Yes
15885	RCT	Augusta	GA	$6,784,521	Black American	3,310	Yes
24683	UNITED NEIGHBORHOOD	Augusta	GA	$1,893,565	Black American	745	Yes
4425	GEORGIA COASTAL	Brunswick	GA	$14,319,988	Asian American, Black American, Hispanic American	1,836	Yes
11489	GOLDEN	Columbus	GA	$397,056	Black American	173	No
24234	OMEGA PSI PHI FRATERNITY	Decatur	GA	$916,490	Black American	827	Yes
24631	PLATINUM	Lilburn	GA	$61,402,761	Asian American	7,220	No
67688	MACON-BIBB EMPLOYEES CREDIT UNION	Macon	GA	$3,532,636	Black American	1,434	No
6582	SAVASTATE TEACHERS	Savannah	GA	$3,461,913	Black American	723	Yes
9527	F A B CHURCH	Savannah	GA	$273,416	Black American	245	Yes
67364	SAVANNAH POSTAL	Savannah	GA	$19,308,617	Black American	2,304	No

CHARTER	NAME	CITY	STATE	ASSETS	MINORITY TYPE	MEMBERS	LOW INCOME
5540	PINEY GROVE COMMUNITY	Swainsboro	GA	$52,740	Black American	63	Yes
22672	RABUN-TALLULAH	Tiger	GA	$591,737	Native American	180	No
20890	STEPHENS COUNTY COMMUNITY	Toccoa	GA	$155,666	Black American	116	Yes
12291	GEORGIA POWER VALDOSTA	Valdosta	GA	$24,502,871	Asian American, Black American, Hispanic American	3,526	No
Total No. of Minority Depository Institutions for Georgia: 20				**$255,775,470**		**58,453**	

HAWAII MINORITY DEPOSITORY INSTITUTIONS

CHARTER	NAME	CITY	STATE	ASSETS	MINORITY TYPE	MEMBERS	LOW INCOME
2713	MCBRYDE	Eleele	HI	$84,129,500	Asian American	3,393	Yes
1987	EWA	Ewa Beach	HI	$12,704,525	Asian American	1,858	Yes
7594	HONEA	Fort Shafter	HI	$25,225,589	Asian American	1,002	Yes
1607	BIG ISLAND	Hilo	HI	$81,186,468	Asian American	8,766	Yes
5628	INDEPENDENT EMPLOYERS GROUP	Hilo	HI	$20,356,867	Asian American, Native American	2,811	Yes
24630	CU HAWAII	Hilo	HI	$246,957,571	Asian American	26,020	Yes
10349	NORTH HAWAII COMMUNITY	Honokaa	HI	$18,213,929	Asian American	3,309	Yes
1717	HAWAIIAN TEL	Honolulu	HI	$540,390,288	Asian American	54,669	No
1733	HICKAM	Honolulu	HI	$541,659,076	Asian American, Black American	49,043	No
1785	HAWAII SCHOOLS	Honolulu	HI	$67,734,179	Asian American	5,904	Yes
1830	HONOLULU	Honolulu	HI	$242,623,251	Asian American	15,400	No
1845	ALOHA PACIFIC	Honolulu	HI	$755,435,295	Asian American	41,610	No
1868	OTS EMPLOYEES	Honolulu	HI	$12,724,722	Asian American, Black American, Hispanic American, Native American	2,052	No
1869	HAWAIIAN ELECTRIC EMPLOYEES	Honolulu	HI	$37,609,250	Asian American	2,106	Yes
1870	HAWAII LAW ENFORCEMENT	Honolulu	HI	$156,120,326	Asian American	13,198	No
1880	HONOLULU FIRE DEPARTMENT	Honolulu	HI	$65,376,841	Asian American	5,208	Yes
4676	HAWAII PACIFIC	Honolulu	HI	$47,135,465	Asian American, Native American	6,162	Yes
5099	THE QUEEN'S	Honolulu	HI	$53,216,501	Asian American	5,173	Yes
5368	PACIFIC ISLAND ENERGY	Honolulu	HI	$7,825,811	Asian American	813	Yes
5927	HAWAIIAN AIRLINES	Honolulu	HI	$19,319,878	Asian American	3,358	Yes
6663	ORAL	Honolulu	HI	$2,514,442	Asian American	324	No
7521	NAVFAC	Honolulu	HI	$30,110,818	Asian American	2,241	Yes
9115	HOTEL AND TRAVEL INDUSTRY	Honolulu	HI	$32,633,205	Asian American	5,060	Yes
9719	ST. FRANCIS MEDICAL CENTER	Honolulu	HI	$9,749,890	Asian American	1,190	No
10465	UNIVERSITY OF HAWAII	Honolulu	HI	$554,130,347	Asian American	29,170	No
10882	LOCAL UNION 1186 IBEW	Honolulu	HI	$14,445,888	Native American	1,176	No

CHARTER	NAME	CITY	STATE	ASSETS	MINORITY TYPE	MEMBERS	LOW INCOME
11332	LEAHI	Honolulu	HI	$1,992,540	Asian American	580	Yes
11494	KUAKINI MEDICAL AND DENTAL	Honolulu	HI	$44,307,997	Asian American	2,721	Yes
11553	KAMEHAMEHA	Honolulu	HI	$38,049,987	Asian American	4,660	No
13158	HAWAII NATIONAL GUARD	Honolulu	HI	$20,075,608	Asian American	2,262	Yes
20187	PRINCE KUHIO	Honolulu	HI	$9,095,822	Black American, Hispanic American	1,544	Yes
24830	OAHU	Honolulu	HI	$49,728,125	Asian American	4,473	No
24839	HAWAII CENTRAL	Honolulu	HI	$190,802,124	Asian American	14,855	No
2275	KAHUKU	Kahuku	HI	$4,843,918	Asian American	1,356	Yes
2562	MAUI	Kahului	HI	$96,622,757	Asian American	7,824	No
3574	VALLEY ISLE COMMUNITY	Kahului	HI	$108,625,485	Asian American, Black American, Hispanic American	12,750	Yes
9924	WAILUKU	Kahului	HI	$41,822,914	Asian American	3,899	Yes
10399	KAHULUI	Kahului	HI	$56,096,714	Asian American, Black American, Hispanic American	4,920	Yes
10938	HAWAII FIRST	Kamuela	HI	$32,234,768	Native American	7,376	Yes
7471	MOLOKAI COMMUNITY	Kaunakakai	HI	$20,411,629	Native American	3,897	Yes
2563	WEST MAUI COMMUNITY	Lahaina	HI	$35,094,516	Asian American	2,680	Yes
2953	LANAI	Lanai City	HI	$26,508,127	Asian American	1,853	Yes
5487	KAUAI GOVERNMENT EMPLOYEES	Lihue	HI	$107,200,708	Black American, Hispanic American	7,161	Yes
2280	HAMAKUA COAST COMMUNITY	Pepeekeo	HI	$15,893,600	Asian American	2,040	Yes
1817	MAUI TEACHERS	Wailuku	HI	$34,119,060	Asian American	1,757	Yes
1961	PEARL HARBOR	Waipahu	HI	$340,868,137	Asian American	25,449	Yes
Total No. of Minority Depository Institutions for Hawaii: 46				**$4,953,924,458**		**405,073**	

ILLINOIS MINORITY DEPOSITORY INSTITUTIONS

CHARTER	NAME	CITY	STATE	ASSETS	MINORITY TYPE	MEMBERS	LOW INCOME
63286	FOX VALLEY	Aurora	IL	$19,688,520	Black American, Hispanic American	2,679	Yes
2467	NORTHSIDE L	Broadview	IL	$8,468,043	Black American	2,292	Yes
2495	CHICAGO AVENUE GARAGE	Chicago	IL	$7,279,325	Black American	883	Yes
2505	77TH STREET DEPOT	Chicago	IL	$18,996,317	Black American, Hispanic American	4,325	Yes
7256	COMMUNITY	Chicago	IL	$133,058	Black American	224	Yes
13533	CTA SOUTH	Chicago	IL	$1,182,063	Black American	624	Yes
14058	ST. MARTIN DE PORRES PARISH	Chicago	IL	$189,928	Black American	125	Yes
15240	RESURRECTION LUTHERAN	Chicago	IL	$183,959	Black American	107	Yes
15454	SHILOH ENGLEWOOD	Chicago	IL	$259,379	Black American	155	Yes
15673	ISRAEL METHCOMM	Chicago	IL	$1,159,147	Black American	230	Yes

CHARTER	NAME	CITY	STATE	ASSETS	MINORITY TYPE	MEMBERS	LOW INCOME
18882	C T A F C	Chicago	IL	$1,041,008	Black American	412	Yes
23245	TRINITY U.C.C.	Chicago	IL	$3,185,879	Black American	966	Yes
24123	M.W.P.H. GRAND LODGE OF ILLINOIS	Chicago	IL	$459,808	Black American	472	Yes
24188	COSMOPOLITAN	Chicago	IL	$96,535	Black American	124	Yes
24704	SOUTH SIDE COMMUNITY	Chicago	IL	$3,331,099	Black American	1,550	Yes
60923	PARK MANOR CHRISTIAN CHURCH	Chicago	IL	$892,783	Black American	354	Yes
61448	ETHICON SUTURE	Chicago	IL	$1,133,859	Hispanic American	554	No
61566	ST. MARK	Chicago	IL	$676,742	Black American	342	Yes
62497	MAROON FINANCIAL	Chicago	IL	$45,828,421	Black American, Hispanic American	6,204	Yes
64252	FELLOWSHIP BAPTIST CHURCH	Chicago	IL	$456,341	Black American	441	Yes
65231	PILGRIM BAPTIST	Chicago	IL	$407,763	Black American	188	Yes
65232	ST. ELIZABETH'S	Chicago	IL	$284,520	Black American	194	No
65433	GREATER INSTITUTIONAL A.M.E. CHURCH	Chicago	IL	$61,666	Black American	99	Yes
65932	CHICAGO MUNICIPAL EMPLOYEES	Chicago	IL	$38,502,480	Black American, Hispanic American	16,951	No
66089	BEREAN	Chicago	IL	$99,302	Black American	236	Yes
66296	ST. HELENA PARISH	Chicago	IL	$87,975	Black American	229	Yes
65640	HEIGHTS AUTO WORKERS	Chicago Heights	IL	$37,579,717	Asian American, Black American, Hispanic American, Native American	6,748	No
20179	ANTIOCH MB	Decatur	IL	$135,576	Black American	160	No
60185	MOTOR COACH EMP.	East Saint Louis	IL	$2,078,221	Black American	1,397	Yes
2498	74TH STREET DEPOT	Evergreen Park	IL	$8,518,264	Black American	726	Yes
2566	BEVERLY BUS GARAGE	Evergreen Park	IL	$3,841,405	Black American	1,200	Yes
61354	GENERAL MILLS EMPLOYEES	Lansing	IL	$14,330,354	Hispanic American	1,451	No
64920	ISU	Normal	IL	$91,589,351	Black American, Hispanic American	10,368	No
2370	METROPOLITAN "L"	Oak Park	IL	$7,020,766	Black American	1,785	Yes
66300	IMPERIAL	Springfield	IL	$38,686	Black American	185	Yes
68472	CANAAN	Urbana	IL	$296,691	Black American	453	Yes
15812	SHILOH BAPTIST	Waukegan	IL	$332,379	Black American	171	Yes
24614	GIDEON	Waukegan	IL	$252,963	Black American	272	Yes
67024	MT. ZION	Zion	IL	$239,584	Black American	265	Yes
Total No. of Minority Depository Institutions for Illinois: 39				**$320,339,877**		**66,141**	

INDIANA MINORITY DEPOSITORY INSTITUTIONS

CHARTER	NAME	CITY	STATE	ASSETS	MINORITY TYPE	MEMBERS	LOW INCOME

CHARTER	NAME	CITY	STATE	ASSETS	MINORITY TYPE	MEMBERS	LOW INCOME
24781	UNION BAPTIST CHURCH	Fort Wayne	IN	$225,765	Black American	303	Yes
169	GARY FIREFIGHTERS ASSOCIATION	Gary	IN	$2,117,066	Black American	394	Yes
3251	GARY POLICE DEPARTMENT EMPLOYEES	Gary	IN	$1,633,043	Black American	372	No
8295	ST. MONICA	Gary	IN	$217,615	Black American	190	Yes
16126	GARY MUNICIPAL EMPLOYEES	Gary	IN	$451,870	Black American	176	Yes
15757	MT ZION INDIANAPOLIS	Indianapolis	IN	$843,636	Black American	382	Yes
2711	PROFINANCE	Merrillville	IN	$14,104,224	Black American	1,979	Yes
6204	RIVER BEND	South Bend	IN	$5,152,600	Black American, Hispanic American	934	Yes
Total No. of Minority Depository Institutions for Indiana: 8				**$24,745,819**		**4,730**	

KANSAS MINORITY DEPOSITORY INSTITUTIONS

CHARTER	NAME	CITY	STATE	ASSETS	MINORITY TYPE	MEMBERS	LOW INCOME
8216	QUINDARO HOMES	Kansas City	KS	$1,379,612	Asian American, Black American, Native American	253	Yes
Total No. of Minority Depository Institutions for Kansas: 1				**$1,379,612**		**253**	

KENTUCKY MINORITY DEPOSITORY INSTITUTIONS

CHARTER	NAME	CITY	STATE	ASSETS	MINORITY TYPE	MEMBERS	LOW INCOME
11487	1ST SELECT	Hopkinsville	KY	$1,034,611	Black American	275	Yes
20595	MSD	Louisville	KY	$4,802,207	Black American	861	Yes
Total No. of Minority Depository Institutions for Kentucky: 2				**$5,836,818**		**1,136**	

LOUISIANA MINORITY DEPOSITORY INSTITUTIONS

CHARTER	NAME	CITY	STATE	ASSETS	MINORITY TYPE	MEMBERS	LOW INCOME
12225	RAPIDES	Alexandria	LA	$6,440,512	Black American	1,227	Yes
2068	SOUTHERN TEACHERS & PARENTS	Baton Rouge	LA	$28,682,226	Black American	5,195	Yes
7253	EAST BATON ROUGE TEACHERS	Baton Rouge	LA	$3,236,408	Black American	1,899	Yes
23899	A M E CHURCH	Baton Rouge	LA	$99,375	Black American	336	Yes
62148	POSTAL	Baton Rouge	LA	$27,495,946	Black American	3,899	No
14225	S M P E	Breaux Bridge	LA	$496,502	Black American	219	Yes
7301	UNION	Farmerville	LA	$1,071,100	Black American	636	Yes
17396	CONCORDIA PARISH SCHOOL EMP	Ferriday	LA	$3,916,289	Black American	1,256	Yes
22417	ST. MARY PARISH SCHOOL EMP.	Franklin	LA	$402,238	Black American	240	Yes
16256	WASHINGTON EDUCATIONAL ASSOC	Franklinton	LA	$966,748	Black American	375	Yes
13248	S H P E	Greensburg	LA	$2,415,540	Black American	1,085	Yes
14692	ASI	Harahan	LA	$312,639,356	Black American, Hispanic American	70,319	Yes
18462	T E A	Houma	LA	$1,988,076	Black American	684	Yes

14537	JAMES WARD, JR.	Jennings	LA	$2,133,827	Black American	422	Yes
63143	IMMACULATE HEART OF MARY	Lafayette	LA	$886,908	Black American	365	Yes
65780	COGIC	Lafayette	LA	$310,979	Black American	420	Yes
62756	SOUTHWEST LOUISIANA	Lake Charles	LA	$79,965,047	Black American	15,620	Yes
15089	S T S P	Mandeville	LA	$645,675	Black American	348	No
23607	WEST JEFFERSON	Marrero	LA	$5,848,048	Black American	1,848	No
7376	FLEUR-DE-LIS	Metairie	LA	$16,391,672	Black American	2,239	Yes
11928	WEBSTER UNITED	Minden	LA	$3,981,435	Black American	1,244	Yes
22219	U B C SOUTHERN COUNCIL INDUSTRIA WO	Minden	LA	$663,869	Black American	379	Yes
62935	MONROE	Monroe	LA	$3,651,166	Black American, Hispanic American	1,087	Yes
4416	IBERIA PARISH	New Iberia	LA	$462,859	Black American	257	Yes
267	U S VETERANS ADMINISTRATION, NEW OR	New Orleans	LA	$1,712,868	Black American	422	No
2056	SEWERAGE & WATER BOARD EMPLOYEES	New Orleans	LA	$6,948,754	Black American	2,209	Yes
5839	SOUTHEAST LOUISIANA VETERANS HEALTH	New Orleans	LA	$1,762,218	Black American	932	Yes
12748	XAVIER UNIVERSITY	New Orleans	LA	$2,369,824	Black American	495	Yes
15588	G G W	New Orleans	LA	$768,200	Black American	227	Yes
19985	ARABI SUGAR WORKERS	New Orleans	LA	$1,282,735	Black American	215	Yes
20550	TEAMSTERS LOCAL UNION #270	New Orleans	LA	$683,448	Black American	438	No
22581	TOTAL COMMUNITY ACTION	New Orleans	LA	$1,317,984	Black American	546	Yes
23540	TULANE/LOYOLA	New Orleans	LA	$19,398,049	Black American	4,336	Yes
60842	NAS JRB	New Orleans	LA	$29,355,949	Asian American, Black American, Hispanic American, Native American	5,286	No
65659	MICHOUD	New Orleans	LA	$4,548,140	Black American	1,094	Yes
66259	ORLEANS PARISH CRIMINAL SHERIFF'S	New Orleans	LA	$6,413,739	Black American	714	No
16386	POINTE COUPEE EDUCATION ASSOC	New Roads	LA	$971,224	Black American	315	Yes
15261	ST. LANDRY PARISH	Opelousas	LA	$6,820,668	Black American, Hispanic American	3,575	Yes
12356	IBERVILLE	Plaquemine	LA	$5,654,032	Black American	3,135	Yes
19452	ST. JOHN SELF-HELP	Reserve	LA	$1,436,795	Black American	330	No
6109	CARVER BRANCH	Shreveport	LA	$663,749	Black American	231	Yes
11658	AVENUE BAPTIST BROTHERHOOD	Shreveport	LA	$505,608	Black American	98	Yes
15589	CADDO PARISH TEACHERS	Shreveport	LA	$10,842,175	Black American	2,757	Yes
13687	FELICIANA	Zachary	LA	$25,514,796	Black American	2,694	Yes

MARYLAND MINORITY DEPOSITORY INSTITUTIONS

CHARTER	NAME	CITY	STATE	ASSETS	MINORITY TYPE	MEMBERS	LOW INCOME
2769	SECURITYPLUS	Baltimore	MD	$359,262,894	Black American	34,724	Yes
20038	THE MOUNT LEBANON	Baltimore	MD	$551,695	Black American	332	Yes
66787	MUNICIPAL EMPL.CREDIT UNION OF BALT	Baltimore	MD	$1,220,294,193	Black American	111,193	Yes
18271	PRINCE GEORGE'S COMMUNITY	Bowie	MD	$144,445,222	Black American, Hispanic American	15,335	No
24778	REID TEMPLE	Glenn Dale	MD	$1,533,544	Black American	1,332	No
7264	MONEY ONE	Largo	MD	$106,889,092	Asian American, Black American, Hispanic American, Native American	12,605	No
22700	KOREAN CATHOLIC	Olney	MD	$1,618,606	Asian American	365	No
22652	CAPITAL AREA TAIWANESE	Rockville	MD	$8,596,145	Asian American	380	No
24246	MT. JEZREEL	Silver Spring	MD	$202,918	Black American	363	Yes
5754	ANDREWS FEDERAL CREDIT UNION	Suitland	MD	$1,060,861,546	Black American	114,561	No
24657	NONE SUFFER LACK	Suitland	MD	$17,104,201	Black American	3,268	No
23484	G.B.B.R.	Timonium	MD	$7,807,225	Asian American, Black American, Hispanic American	1,596	No
Total No. of Minority Depository Institutions for Maryland: 12				**$2,929,167,281**		**296,054**	

MASSACHUSETTS MINORITY DEPOSITORY INSTITUTIONS

CHARTER	NAME	CITY	STATE	ASSETS	MINORITY TYPE	MEMBERS	LOW INCOME
11400	GOLDMARK	Attleboro	MA	$29,235,447	Asian American, Black American, Hispanic American, Native American	3,382	No
16383	NEW ENGLAND LEE	Boston	MA	$3,911,055	Asian American	326	No
24043	MESSIAH BAPTIST-JUBILEE	Brockton	MA	$601,257	Black American	400	Yes
Total No. of Minority Depository Institutions for Massachusetts: 3				**$33,747,759**		**4,108**	

MICHIGAN MINORITY DEPOSITORY INSTITUTIONS

CHARTER	NAME	CITY	STATE	ASSETS	MINORITY TYPE	MEMBERS	LOW INCOME
19730	2ND BAPTIST CH. OF ANN ARBOR	Ann Arbor	MI	$110,405	Black American	219	No
24030	NEW RISING STAR	Detroit	MI	$108,931	Black American	168	Yes
60993	METROPOLITAN CHURCH OF GOD	Detroit	MI	$145,837	Black American	198	Yes
61375	FANNIE B. PECK OF BETHEL AME CHURCH	Detroit	MI	$609,523	Black American	500	No
61907	VETERANS HEALTH ADMINISTRATION	Detroit	MI	$3,173,210	Black American	1,289	No
62167	I.M. DETROIT DISTRICT	Detroit	MI	$1,438,445	Black American	305	No

62177	BETHEL BAPTIST CHURCH EAST	Detroit	MI	$634,136	Black American	320	No
62324	GREATER NEW MT. MORIAH BAPTIST CHRH	Detroit	MI	$296,024	Black American	212	No
63106	HEALTH ONE	Detroit	MI	$16,669,942	Black American	3,764	No
63713	GREATER CHRIST BAPTIST CHURCH	Detroit	MI	$741,514	Black American	385	No
19197	FOSS AVENUE BAPTIST CHURCH	Flint	MI	$257,989	Black American	298	Yes
61641	FM FINANCIAL	Flint	MI	$33,041,806	Black American	4,778	Yes
61678	MUSKEGON CONSUMERS POWER EMPLOYEES	Muskegon	MI	$5,589,021	Black American, Hispanic American	1,115	No
23012	BETHEL A.M.E. CHURCH	Saginaw	MI	$1,078,983	Black American	684	Yes
7628	SOUTHEAST MICHIGAN STATE EMPLOYEES	Southfield	MI	$32,011,847	Black American	4,459	Yes
4787	TANDEM	Warren	MI	$21,794,258	Black American, Hispanic American	3,005	Yes
5885	A.B.D.	Warren	MI	$61,797,506	Black American	13,731	Yes
Total No. of Minority Depository Institutions for Michigan: 17				**$179,499,377**		**35,430**	

MINNESOTA MINORITY DEPOSITORY INSTITUTIONS

CHARTER	NAME	CITY	STATE	ASSETS	MINORITY TYPE	MEMBERS	LOW INCOME
17749	WHITE EARTH RESERVATION	Mahnomen	MN	$1,642,192	Native American	1,606	Yes
24852	NORTHERN EAGLE	Nett Lake	MN	$349,219	Native American	224	Yes
Total No. of Minority Depository Institutions for Minnesota: 2				**$1,991,411**		**1,830**	

MISSISSIPPI MINORITY DEPOSITORY INSTITUTIONS

CHARTER	NAME	CITY	STATE	ASSETS	MINORITY TYPE	MEMBERS	LOW INCOME
9974	SHELBY/BOLIVAR COUNTY	Boyle	MS	$2,057,915	Black American	2,030	Yes
22314	CHOCTAW	Choctaw	MS	$1,984,250	Native American	1,966	Yes
63869	STEPHENS-ADAMSON EMPLOYEES	Clarksdale	MS	$132,763	Black American	41	No
61784	ELLISVILLE STATE SCHOOL EMPLOYEES	Ellisville	MS	$2,315,863	Black American	600	No
14193	FORREST COUNTY TEACHERS	Hattiesburg	MS	$240,492	Black American	357	Yes
62864	MID DELTA	Indianola	MS	$1,669,329	Black American	2,082	Yes
7684	JPFCE	Jackson	MS	$1,065,033	Black American	183	Yes
8052	MISSISSIPPI DHS	Jackson	MS	$7,554,361	Black American	2,590	Yes
8445	JACKSON AREA	Jackson	MS	$63,400,381	Black American	12,269	Yes
9567	MBHS	Jackson	MS	$9,098,648	Black American	2,221	Yes
24585	MISSISSIPPI	Jackson	MS	$101,412,206	Black American	14,596	Yes
24829	HOPE	Jackson	MS	$182,053,880	Black American	29,515	Yes
63442	MISSISSIPPI PUBLIC EMPLOYEES	Jackson	MS	$21,320,590	Black American	6,829	Yes
19253	ISSAQUENA COUNTY	Mayersville	MS	$1,202,674	Black American	462	Yes
24859	FIRST UNITY	McComb	MS	$122,453	Black American	1	Yes

8433	MERIDIAN MUTUAL	Meridian	MS	$32,972,775	Black American	6,609	Yes
17715	CITIZENS CHOICE	Natchez	MS	$1,145,391	Black American	459	Yes
22414	T.P.C. EMPLOYEES	Tupelo	MS	$457,490	Black American	215	Yes
18436	CENTRAL MISSISSIPPI	Winona	MS	$362,387	Black American	234	Yes
Total No. of Minority Depository Institutions for Mississippi: 19				**$430,568,881**		**83,259**	

MISSOURI MINORITY DEPOSITORY INSTITUTIONS

CHARTER	NAME	CITY	STATE	ASSETS	MINORITY TYPE	MEMBERS	LOW INCOME
4531	KC TERMINAL EMPL/ GUADALUPE CENTER	Kansas City	MO	$2,107,988	Hispanic American	990	Yes
61459	CROSS ROADS	Kansas City	MO	$4,689,451	Black American, Hispanic American	1,388	Yes
63388	KANSAS CITY	Kansas City	MO	$28,639,298	Black American	6,620	No
21683	WEST SIDE BAPTIST CHURCH	Saint Louis	MO	$307,633	Black American	400	Yes
60400	ST. LOUIS COMMUNITY	Saint Louis	MO	$238,709,693	Black American	48,331	Yes
64425	ST. LOUIS POLICEMEN`S	Saint Louis	MO	$19,564,212	Black American	2,384	No
67744	UNION MEMORIAL	Saint Louis	MO	$196,935	Black American	156	Yes
Total No. of Minority Depository Institutions for Missouri: 7				**$294,215,210**		**60,269**	

MONTANA MINORITY DEPOSITORY INSTITUTIONS

CHARTER	NAME	CITY	STATE	ASSETS	MINORITY TYPE	MEMBERS	LOW INCOME
15375	WOLF POINT	Wolf Point	MT	$12,049,871	Native American	2,504	Yes
Total No. of Minority Depository Institutions for Montana: 1				**$12,049,871**		**2,504**	

NEVADA MINORITY DEPOSITORY INSTITUTIONS

CHARTER	NAME	CITY	STATE	ASSETS	MINORITY TYPE	MEMBERS	LOW INCOME
7698	LAS VEGAS UP EMPLOYEES	Las Vegas	NV	$4,773,357	Asian American, Black American, Hispanic American, Native American	916	No
Total No. of Minority Depository Institutions for Nevada: 1				**$4,773,357**		**916**	

NEW JERSEY MINORITY DEPOSITORY INSTITUTIONS

CHARTER	NAME	CITY	STATE	ASSETS	MINORITY TYPE	MEMBERS	LOW INCOME
3879	W. K.	Belleville	NJ	$963,548	Asian American, Black American, Hispanic American	238	Yes
66276	FIRST BAPTIST CHURCH CRANFORD NJ	Cranford	NJ	$105,811	Black American	176	No
21440	MESSIAH BAPTIST CHURCH	East Orange	NJ	$281,307	Black American	218	Yes
4738	ATLANTIC COUNTY NJ EMPLOYEES	Egg Harbor Town	NJ	$2,698,314	Asian American, Black American, Hispanic American	663	No
14329	UNION COUNTY EMPLOYEES	Elizabeth	NJ	$8,526,189	Asian American, Black American, Hispanic American	2,029	No

CHARTER	NAME	CITY	STATE	ASSETS	MINORITY TYPE	MEMBERS	LOW INCOME
11895	BETHANY BAPTIST	Farmingdale	NJ	$8,257	Black American, Native American	5	No
22449	NESTLE (FREEHOLD) EMPLOYEES	Freehold	NJ	$2,470,717	Hispanic American	233	No
1546	MERCER COUNTY IMPROVEMENT AUTHORITY	Hamilton	NJ	$389,182	Black American	236	Yes
62855	DIVISION 819 TRANSIT EMPLOYEES	Irvington	NJ	$21,522,435	Black American	1,857	No
23265	HELPING OTHER PEOPLE EXCEL	Jackson	NJ	$77,605	Black American	116	Yes
5987	OCNAC #1	Jersey City	NJ	$6,232,344	Black American, Hispanic American	2,302	Yes
7184	LIBERTY SAVINGS	Jersey City	NJ	$79,658,293	Asian American, Black American, Hispanic American	20,078	Yes
15154	SALEM BAPTIST	Jersey City	NJ	$127,792	Black American	107	Yes
112	ESSEX COUNTY NJ EMPLOYEES	Newark	NJ	$6,462,442	Black American, Hispanic American	2,135	Yes
10803	ISRAEL MEMORIAL A M E	Newark	NJ	$672,818	Black American	260	No
20773	LOCAL 1233	Newark	NJ	$9,327,796	Black American	673	No
24167	NEW COMMUNITY	Newark	NJ	$3,259,726	Black American, Hispanic American	3,233	Yes
62796	NEWARK BOARD OF EDUCATION EMPLOYEES	Newark	NJ	$37,383,473	Asian American, Black American	5,610	No
66159	NEWARK POST OFFICE EMPLOYEES	Newark	NJ	$3,475,451	Black American	1,158	No
24115	ST. ANDREW KIM	Palisades Park	NJ	$2,269,465	Asian American	705	No
12227	PASSAIC POLICE	Passaic	NJ	$4,930,191	Hispanic American	543	No
2892	PLAINFIELD POLICE & FIREMEN'S	Plainfield	NJ	$4,374,007	Black American	548	No
23615	HEARD A.M.E.	Roselle	NJ	$258,439	Black American	195	Yes
23678	GOYA FOODS EMPLOYEES	Secaucus	NJ	$9,949,681	Hispanic American	823	No
68195	RENAISSANCE COMMUNITY DEVELOPMENT C	Somerset	NJ	$808,507	Black American, Hispanic American, Native American	700	Yes
15139	BERGEN DIVISION	Toms River	NJ	$8,238,365	Black American, Hispanic American	1,525	No
1015	NORTH JERSEY	Totowa	NJ	$219,868,942	Asian American, Black American, Hispanic American	30,338	Yes
18546	MOUNT ZION A M E CHURCH	Trenton	NJ	$56,386	Black American	108	Yes
63512	CITY OF TRENTON EMPLOYEES	Trenton	NJ	$1,243,282	Black American, Hispanic American	533	No
9723	N.J.T. EMPLOYEES	Waldwick	NJ	$11,148,300	Black American, Hispanic American	1,042	No
Total No. of Minority Depository Institutions for New Jersey: 30				**$446,789,065**		**78,387**	

NEW MEXICO MINORITY DEPOSITORY INSTITUTIONS

CHARTER	NAME	CITY	STATE	ASSETS	MINORITY TYPE	MEMBERS	LOW INCOME
808	U.S. NEW MEXICO	Albuquerque	NM	$803,410,668	Asian American, Black American, Hispanic American, Native American	74,856	No

964	SOUTHWEST	Albuquerque	NM	$55,406,927	Hispanic American, Native American	5,052	No
62573	RIO GRANDE	Albuquerque	NM	$243,507,435	Asian American, Black American, Hispanic American, Native American	26,784	No
9566	EDDY	Carlsbad	NM	$60,855,448	Hispanic American	6,593	No
61946	RINCONES PRESBYTERIAN	Chacon	NM	$3,279,059	Hispanic American	681	Yes
66097	CUBA	Cuba	NM	$12,239,249	Hispanic American, Native American	2,050	Yes
16754	FOUR CORNERS	Kirtland	NM	$25,978,867	Native American	5,004	Yes
60467	ZIA	Los Alamos	NM	$129,162,264	Hispanic American	12,706	No
62289	ST. GERTRUDE'S	Mora	NM	$1,775,153	Hispanic American	613	Yes
66252	QUESTA	Questa	NM	$7,214,099	Hispanic American	892	Yes
7999	TELCO ROSWELL NEW MEXICO	Roswell	NM	$7,272,814	Hispanic American	1,181	Yes
65513	STATE EMPLOYEES	Santa Fe	NM	$386,820,022	Hispanic American, Native American	37,930	No
66149	GUADALUPE	Santa Fe	NM	$133,262,584	Hispanic American	14,908	Yes
1838	FORT BAYARD	Silver City	NM	$4,707,074	Hispanic American	1,266	Yes
Total No. of Minority Depository Institutions for New Mexico: 14				**$1,874,891,663**		**190,516**	

NEW YORK MINORITY DEPOSITORY INSTITUTIONS

CHARTER	NAME	CITY	STATE	ASSETS	MINORITY TYPE	MEMBERS	LOW INCOME
5263	ST. AUGUSTINE PRESBYTERIAN	Bronx	NY	$108,936	Black American, Hispanic American	125	Yes
19907	BETHEX	Bronx	NY	$17,151,055	Black American, Hispanic American	5,598	Yes
24740	LOVE GOSPEL ASSEMBLY	Bronx	NY	$109,880	Black American, Hispanic American	215	Yes
24784	NEW COVENANT DOMINION	Bronx	NY	$1,206,295	Asian American, Black American, Hispanic American	977	Yes
7504	CONCORD	Brooklyn	NY	$8,530,419	Black American	1,350	Yes
12085	CORNERSTONE BAPTIST CHURCH	Brooklyn	NY	$120,148	Black American	233	Yes
15067	TRANSFIGURATION PARISH	Brooklyn	NY	$7,253,026	Hispanic American	2,355	Yes
15129	EPIPHANY	Brooklyn	NY	$214,728	Hispanic American	83	Yes
15246	PRINCE	Brooklyn	NY	$73,095	Hispanic American	36	Yes
17358	GOOD COUNSEL	Brooklyn	NY	$502,433	Black American, Hispanic American	193	Yes
18858	SPC BROOKLYN	Brooklyn	NY	$475,667	Black American	330	Yes
20419	BYKOTA	Brooklyn	NY	$1,492,967	Black American	960	Yes
23888	BEREA	Brooklyn	NY	$163,961	Black American	316	Yes
24642	BROOKLYN COOPERATIVE	Brooklyn	NY	$19,656,395	Asian American, Black American, Hispanic American	5,740	Yes

24790	BEULAH	Brooklyn	NY	$174,869	Black American	182	Yes
21355	ST. JOHN UNITED	Buffalo	NY	$1,121,403	Black American	1,481	Yes
22226	FIRST BAPTIST CHURCH	East Elmhurst	NY	$388,434	Black American	199	Yes
4246	FAR ROCKAWAY POSTAL	Far Rockaway	NY	$622,674	Black American	99	No
23503	KOREAN AMERICAN CATHOLICS	Flushing	NY	$28,575,145	Asian American	2,836	No
23658	PAUL QUINN	Flushing	NY	$370,036	Black American	180	Yes
24598	VARICK MEMORIAL	Hempstead	NY	$351,382	Black American	254	Yes
22344	QUEENS CLUSTER	Hicksville	NY	$283,316	Black American	77	Yes
20885	MEDISYS EMPLOYEES	Jamaica	NY	$25,783,065	Asian American, Black American, Hispanic American	3,954	No
23317	LAST	Long Island CIT	NY	$169,448	Asian American, Black American, Hispanic American	436	Yes
24823	URBAN UPBOUND	Long Island CIT	NY	$779,236	Black American	1,106	Yes
132	MOUNT VERNON NY POSTAL EMPLOYEES	Mount Vernon	NY	$1,962,938	Black American	409	No
19775	GREATER CENTENNIAL	Mount Vernon	NY	$356,837	Black American	277	Yes
165	NEW YORK STATE EMPLOYEES	New York	NY	$2,225,827	Black American	1,172	Yes
798	TRANSIT AUTHORITY DIVISION B	New York	NY	$5,019,679	Black American, Hispanic American	1,755	No
1343	EMPIRT 207	New York	NY	$3,990,842	Black American, Hispanic American	808	No
2184	ST. MARTIN'S	New York	NY	$214,987	Black American	207	Yes
3714	UNIVERSITY SETTLEMENT	New York	NY	$846,615	Asian American, Hispanic American	191	Yes
4170	ABYSSINIAN BAPTIST CHURCH	New York	NY	$1,125,089	Black American	299	Yes
5022	ST. MARKS	New York	NY	$222,855	Black American, Hispanic American	129	Yes
5127	CHURCH OF THE MASTER	New York	NY	$640,888	Black American	376	Yes
5655	UNION CONGREGATION-AL	New York	NY	$370,699	Black American	138	Yes
7172	ST. PHILIP'S CHURCH	New York	NY	$1,642,374	Black American	416	Yes
8950	ALL SOULS	New York	NY	$271,393	Black American	185	Yes
11380	FIDELIS	New York	NY	$332,502	Black American	304	Yes
16532	BOOTSTRAP	New York	NY	$798,922	Hispanic American	48	No
20060	N.U.L.	New York	NY	$432,484	Black American	83	Yes
20495	TRANSFIGURATION MANHATTAN	New York	NY	$112,344	Black American, Hispanic American	146	Yes
22032	ENTERTAINMENT INDUSTRIES	New York	NY	$13,565,636	Black American, Hispanic American	1,980	Yes
23177	SOUTHERN BAPTIST CHURCH OF NEW YORK	New York	NY	$221,437	Black American	105	Yes
23958	NEW YORK UNIVERSITY	New York	NY	$14,811,543	Asian American, Black American, Hispanic American	4,196	Yes

23967	65 FAMILY	New York	NY	$2,523,857	Black American, Hispanic American	1,046	Yes
24232	LOWER EAST SIDE PEOPLE'S	New York	NY	$42,904,152	Black American, Hispanic American	8,390	Yes
24670	1199 SEIU	New York	NY	$60,715,854	Asian American, Black American, Hispanic American	28,495	Yes
60153	MUNICIPAL	New York	NY	$2,035,964,122	Asian American, Black American, Hispanic American, Native American	357,743	No
63906	EMPIRE BR 36 NATL ASSOC OF LE CARR	New York	NY	$5,392,644	Asian American, Black American, Hispanic American	1,333	No
18528	SAINT JOHN A M E	Niagara Falls	NY	$193,325	Black American, Hispanic American	202	Yes
4441	SING SING EMPLOYEES	Ossining	NY	$6,507,547	Hispanic American	1,361	Yes
15080	ROCKLAND EMPLOYEES	Spring Valley	NY	$28,483,466	Black American, Hispanic American	5,385	No
21831	TRANSIT	Valley Stream	NY	$14,441,480	Asian American, Black American, Hispanic American	4,772	Yes
16790	UNION BAPTIST GREENBURGH	White Plains	NY	$320,138	Black American	297	Yes
63918	YONKERS POSTAL EMPLOYEES	Yonkers	NY	$7,808,767	Black American	511	No
Total No. of Minority Depository Institutions for New York: 56				**$2,370,099,256**		**452,074**	

NORTH CAROLINA MINORITY DEPOSITORY INSTITUTIONS

CHARTER	NAME	CITY	STATE	ASSETS	MINORITY TYPE	MEMBERS	LOW INCOME
68593	FIRST LEGACY COMMUNITY	Charlotte	NC	$36,310,897	Black American	10,189	Yes
24802	SELF-HELP	Durham	NC	$550,792,712	Hispanic American	49,734	Yes
63595	MOUNT VERNON BAPTIST CHURCH	Durham	NC	$192,127	Black American	300	No
68430	LATINO COMMUNITY	Durham	NC	$150,512,421	Hispanic American	54,710	Yes
3685	INTERNAL REVENUE EMPLOYEES	Greensboro	NC	$24,358,000	Black American	1,210	No
64034	GREATER KINSTON	Kinston	NC	$10,706,054	Black American	5,641	Yes
19826	SHAW UNIVERSITY	Raleigh	NC	$522,391	Black American	130	Yes
Total No. of Minority Depository Institutions for North Carolina: 7				**$773,394,602**		**121,914**	

OHIO MINORITY DEPOSITORY INSTITUTIONS

CHARTER	NAME	CITY	STATE	ASSETS	MINORITY TYPE	MEMBERS	LOW INCOME
24646	STARK METROPOLITAN HOUSING AUTHORITY	Canton	OH	$1,774,139	Black American	1,558	Yes
6207	CARMEL BROTHERHOOD	Cincinnati	OH	$236,851	Black American	146	Yes
18562	MT ZION WOODLAWN	Cincinnati	OH	$98,460	Black American	341	Yes
13149	GREATER ABYSSINIA	Cleveland	OH	$580,994	Black American	448	Yes
17555	STEEL VALLEY	Cleveland	OH	$37,128,407	Black American, Hispanic American	9,162	Yes
22151	CLEVELAND CHURCH OF CHRIST	Cleveland	OH	$216,552	Black American	547	Yes
61622	CORY METHODIST CHURCH	Cleveland	OH	$1,881,938	Black American	661	Yes

CHARTER	NAME	CITY	STATE	ASSETS	MINORITY TYPE	MEMBERS	LOW INCOME
66860	CIVIL SERVICE EMPLOYEES ASSOCIATION	Cleveland	OH	$6,214,494	Black American	2,689	No
14798	BETHEL COMMUNITY	Dayton	OH	$210,686	Asian American, Black American, Hispanic American	230	Yes
2538	RTA HAYDEN	E Cleveland	OH	$1,692,624	Black American	733	Yes
21226	PROMEDICA	Toledo	OH	$50,941,990	Asian American, Black American, Hispanic American	7,061	Yes
24578	TOLEDO URBAN	Toledo	OH	$4,540,073	Black American	2,037	Yes
68603	NUEVA ESPERANZA COMMUNITY	Toledo	OH	$1,569,714	Hispanic American, Native American	433	Yes
14469	YHA SOUTH UNIT	Youngstown	OH	$1,781,307	Black American	611	Yes
Total No. of Minority Depository Institutions for Ohio: 14				**$108,868,229**		**26,657**	

OKLAHOMA MINORITY DEPOSITORY INSTITUTIONS

CHARTER	NAME	CITY	STATE	ASSETS	MINORITY TYPE	MEMBERS	LOW INCOME
10283	THE FOCUS	Oklahoma City	OK	$99,397,842	Asian American, Black American, Hispanic American, Native American	10,631	Yes
65774	TEACHERS	Oklahoma City	OK	$6,648,733	Asian American, Black American, Hispanic American, Native American	2,735	No
14610	MORNING STAR	Tulsa	OK	$485,824	Black American	474	Yes
60696	FIRE FIGHTERS	Tulsa	OK	$34,913,496	Black American, Hispanic American, Native American	5,208	No
Total No. of Minority Depository Institutions for Oklahoma: 4				**$141,445,895**		**19,048**	

PENNSYLVANIA MINORITY DEPOSITORY INSTITUTIONS

CHARTER	NAME	CITY	STATE	ASSETS	MINORITY TYPE	MEMBERS	LOW INCOME
3122	CHESTER UPLAND SCHOOL EMPLOYEES	Chester	PA	$920,593	Black American	470	Yes
24016	BETHANY BAPTIST CHRISTIAN	Chester	PA	$80,508	Black American	116	Yes
20839	MORNING STAR BAPTIST	Clairton	PA	$568,626	Black American	379	Yes
23640	FIRST BAPTIST CHURCH OF DARBY	Darby	PA	$62,771	Black American	135	Yes
2822	LANCASTER PA FIREMEN	Lancaster	PA	$905,260	Black American, Hispanic American	432	No
3297	PHILADELPHIA MINT	Philadelphia	PA	$872,924	Black American	399	Yes
11500	ZION	Philadelphia	PA	$288,548	Black American	339	Yes
11783	S I PHILADELPHIA	Philadelphia	PA	$225,688	Black American	167	Yes
13234	S M	Philadelphia	PA	$98,957	Black American	112	Yes
14430	WESLEY AME ZION	Philadelphia	PA	$138,294	Black American	212	Yes
16525	MOUNT CARMEL BAPTIST	Philadelphia	PA	$823,378	Black American	376	Yes

16728	PINN MEMORIAL	Philadelphia	PA	$217,251	Black American	434	Yes
17269	HOLY TRINITY BAPTIST	Philadelphia	PA	$18,413	Black American	81	Yes
17772	HOLSEY TEMPLE	Philadelphia	PA	$39,343	Black American	114	Yes
17885	TRANSIT WORKERS	Philadelphia	PA	$21,077,183	Black American, Hispanic American	5,900	Yes
19046	ST. PAULS	Philadelphia	PA	$121,238	Black American	245	Yes
19770	WARD	Philadelphia	PA	$143,875	Black American	148	Yes
21535	THE TRIUMPH BAPTIST	Philadelphia	PA	$441,451	Black American	361	Yes
22007	WAYLAND TEMPLE BAPTIST	Philadelphia	PA	$227,358	Black American	202	Yes
23037	WHITE ROCK	Philadelphia	PA	$783,289	Black American	147	No
24104	TROUVAILLE	Philadelphia	PA	$1,599,652	Black American, Hispanic American	1,450	Yes
24266	M.A.B.C.	Philadelphia	PA	$133,915	Black American	210	Yes
24853	NEW LIFE	Philadelphia	PA	$587,325	Black American	892	Yes
20354	HILL DISTRICT	Pittsburgh	PA	$4,034,596	Black American	2,974	Yes
61035	SWINDELL-DRESSLER	Pittsburgh	PA	$6,582,516	Asian American, Black American	645	No
10687	HORIZON	Williamsport	PA	$62,376,753	Black American, Hispanic American	9,903	No
4871	E R R L	Wyndmoor	PA	$1,532,371	Black American, Hispanic American	334	No
Total No. of Minority Depository Institutions for Pennsylvania: 27				**$104,902,076**		**27,177**	

PUERTO RICO MINORITY DEPOSITORY INSTITUTIONS

CHARTER	NAME	CITY	STATE	ASSETS	MINORITY TYPE	MEMBERS	LOW INCOME
7347	BORINQUEN COMMUNITY	Aguadilla	PR	$18,115,309	Hispanic American	3,351	Yes
11261	V. SUAREZ EMPLOYEES	Bayamon	PR	$391,491	Hispanic American	200	Yes
14600	GOLMAR	Bayamon	PR	$359,848	Hispanic American	53	No
13939	PUERTO RICO	Caparra	PR	$124,449,750	Hispanic American	20,899	Yes
11246	BORINQUEN SUR	Penuelas	PR	$9,991,066	Hispanic American	3,107	Yes
13785	GLAMOUR COMMUNITY	Quebradillas	PR	$3,283,366	Hispanic American	1,310	Yes
11477	UNIVERSAL COOP	Rio Grande	PR	$20,176,254	Hispanic American	3,632	Yes
6918	VAPR	San Juan	PR	$182,784,294	Hispanic American	15,533	Yes
7345	CARIBE	San Juan	PR	$285,316,001	Hispanic American	24,624	Yes
Total No. of Minority Depository Institutions for Puerto Rico: 9				**$644,867,379**		**72,709**	

SOUTH CAROLINA MINORITY DEPOSITORY INSTITUTIONS

CHARTER	NAME	CITY	STATE	ASSETS	MINORITY TYPE	MEMBERS	LOW INCOME
10875	CHARLESTON COUNTY TEACHERS	Charleston	SC	$1,601,492	Black American	988	Yes
17655	C O	Charleston	SC	$1,776,173	Black American	387	Yes
19619	TRINITY BAPTIST CHURCH	Florence	SC	$2,533,117	Black American	226	Yes

22530	PEE DEE	Florence	SC	$25,623,780	Black American	6,798	Yes
24856	COMMUNITYWORKS	Greenville	SC	$275,177	Black American, Hispanic American	21	No
13472	BERKELEY COMMUNITY	Moncks Corner	SC	$9,791,727	Black American	2,432	Yes
1397	EDISTO	Orangeburg	SC	$25,065,275	Hispanic American, Native American	3,468	Yes
60752	SUMTER CITY	Sumter	SC	$3,063,585	Black American	849	No
24623	BROOKLAND	West Columbia	SC	$3,625,170	Black American	1,356	Yes
Total No. of Minority Depository Institutions for South Carolina: 9				**$73,355,496**		**16,525**	

SOUTH DAKOTA MINORITY DEPOSITORY INSTITUTIONS

CHARTER	NAME	CITY	STATE	ASSETS	MINORITY TYPE	MEMBERS	LOW INCOME
23309	SISSETON-WAHPETON	Agency Village	SD	$4,200,983	Native American	1,890	Yes
24847	LAKOTA	Kyle	SD	$2,297,933	Native American	1,535	Yes
Total No. of Minority Depository Institutions for South Dakota: 2				**$6,498,916**		**3,425**	

TENNESSEE MINORITY DEPOSITORY INSTITUTIONS

CHARTER	NAME	CITY	STATE	ASSETS	MINORITY TYPE	MEMBERS	LOW INCOME
15433	MEMPHIS MUNICIPAL EMPLOYEES	Memphis	TN	$13,009,501	Black American	2,634	Yes
20722	I TRUST	Memphis	TN	$17,762,968	Black American	3,260	No
6667	TSU	Nashville	TN	$1,384,709	Black American	453	Yes
67990	N.G.H.	Nashville	TN	$6,905,707	Black American	3,114	Yes
Total No. of Minority Depository Institutions for Tennessee: 4				**$39,062,885**		**9,461**	

TEXAS MINORITY DEPOSITORY INSTITUTIONS

CHARTER	NAME	CITY	STATE	ASSETS	MINORITY TYPE	MEMBERS	LOW INCOME
68010	ALPINE COMMUNITY	Alpine	TX	$14,943,784	Hispanic American	1,994	Yes
24605	MOUNT OLIVE BAPTIST CHURCH	Arlington	TX	$4,997,881	Black American	1,114	No
15563	BAYCEL	Bay City	TX	$46,182,345	Hispanic American	3,797	No
17105	PEAR ORCHARD	Beaumont	TX	$933,368	Black American	362	Yes
67501	S A F E	Beaumont	TX	$11,382,141	Black American	2,160	Yes
67574	BEAUMONT COMMUNITY	Beaumont	TX	$26,532,768	Black American, Hispanic American	3,863	No
13873	BROWNFIELD	Brownfield	TX	$11,854,530	Black American, Hispanic American	2,595	No
850	VALLEY	Brownsville	TX	$55,800,118	Hispanic American	10,579	No
20392	BROWNSVILLE CITY EMPLOYEES	Brownsville	TX	$6,563,341	Hispanic American	1,558	Yes
21788	VALWOOD PARK	Carrollton	TX	$19,542,210	Black American, Hispanic American	3,999	No
4060	GULF COAST	Corpus Christi	TX	$157,852,232	Hispanic American	10,443	Yes
5450	HOMEPORT	Corpus Christi	TX	$15,849,386	Hispanic American	2,823	Yes
12426	IBEW LU 278	Corpus Christi	TX	$2,516,099	Hispanic American	848	Yes

67578	NCE	Corpus Christi	TX	$4,597,342	Hispanic American	1,149	No
67963	CORPUS CHRISTI POSTAL EMPLOYEES	Corpus Christi	TX	$14,369,345	Hispanic American	2,059	No
68300	SOUTH TEXAS AREA RESOURCES	Corpus Christi	TX	$44,842,864	Hispanic American	5,674	No
68482	COASTAL COMMUNITY AND TEACHERS	Corpus Christi	TX	$280,294,464	Hispanic American	36,581	No
68626	SUNTIDE CREDIT UNION	Corpus Christi	TX	$88,972,589	Hispanic American	8,279	Yes
5497	TEXAS	Dallas	TX	$66,726,732	Asian American, Black American, Hispanic American, Native American	9,347	No
12108	GOOD STREET BAPTIST CHURCH	Dallas	TX	$1,089,336	Black American	679	Yes
12859	FAITH COOPERATIVE	Dallas	TX	$423,027	Black American	448	Yes
22157	SOUTHWEST AIRLINES	Dallas	TX	$334,302,989	Black American, Hispanic American	40,904	No
24804	OAK CLIFF CHRISTIAN	Dallas	TX	$3,730,609	Black American	1,551	No
67413	TEXAS HEALTH RESOURCES	Dallas	TX	$16,769,763	Asian American, Black American, Hispanic American	3,851	No
67669	CITY	Dallas	TX	$282,980,142	Asian American, Black American, Hispanic American	39,054	No
68436	NEW MOUNT ZION BAPTIST CHURCH	Dallas	TX	$965,043	Asian American, Black American, Hispanic American	500	Yes
68439	RESOURCE ONE	Dallas	TX	$393,455,267	Black American, Hispanic American	48,157	No
24304	BORDER	Del Rio	TX	$123,333,853	Asian American, Black American, Hispanic American, Native American	23,801	Yes
5547	SECURITY FIRST	Edinburg	TX	$379,113,443	Hispanic American	56,025	Yes
66366	EDINBURG TEACHERS	Edinburg	TX	$81,171,894	Hispanic American	13,096	Yes
67881	COUNTY & MUNICIPAL EMPLOYEES	Edinburg	TX	$41,887,412	Hispanic American	7,221	No
856	MOUNTAIN STAR	El Paso	TX	$26,798,853	Hispanic American	4,714	Yes
1409	EL PASO AREA TEACHERS	El Paso	TX	$505,768,953	Asian American, Black American, Hispanic American	50,318	Yes
1792	EVOLVE	El Paso	TX	$324,823,286	Hispanic American	39,574	Yes
2115	ONE SOURCE	El Paso	TX	$89,634,576	Hispanic American	11,687	Yes
5929	TIP OF TEXAS	El Paso	TX	$21,981,008	Hispanic American	4,221	Yes
7224	GOLDEN KEY	El Paso	TX	$61,610,928	Hispanic American	5,763	Yes
10174	FIRSTLIGHT	El Paso	TX	$837,443,653	Hispanic American	115,147	Yes
60058	GECU	El Paso	TX	$2,075,029,750	Hispanic American	314,653	Yes
10843	ALL SAINTS CATHOLIC	Fort Worth	TX	$542,051	Hispanic American	165	Yes
9843	FRIONA TEXAS	Friona	TX	$12,162,073	Hispanic American	1,989	Yes
7092	GALVESTON SCHOOL EMPLOYEES	Galveston	TX	$3,919,385	Black American, Hispanic American	1,112	Yes

11927	COASTAL COMMUNITY	Galveston	TX	$49,185,720	Black American, Hispanic American	9,061	Yes
60307	GRAND PRAIRIE	Grand Prairie	TX	$14,506,710	Black American, Hispanic American	2,436	No
61734	RIO GRANDE VALLEY CREDIT UNION	Harlingen	TX	$79,812,287	Hispanic American	16,908	Yes
15817	PILGRIM CUCC	Houston	TX	$1,317,906	Black American	403	Yes
17067	OUR MOTHER OF MERCY PARISH HOUSTON	Houston	TX	$2,561,011	Black American	697	Yes
18218	TEXAS LEE	Houston	TX	$192,437	Asian American	89	No
21029	PORT OF HOUSTON WAREHOUSE	Houston	TX	$4,121,387	Black American	305	No
23328	RIO GRANDE MASONIC PRINCE HALL	Houston	TX	$335,988	Black American	81	No
24324	MET TRAN	Houston	TX	$8,392,657	Black American	2,638	Yes
24463	BRENTWOOD BAPTIST CHURCH	Houston	TX	$915,052	Black American	1,010	Yes
24570	HOUSTON METROPOLITAN	Houston	TX	$43,079,442	Black American, Hispanic American	12,315	Yes
24769	EMPOWERMENT COMMUNITY DEVELOPMENT	Houston	TX	$1,484,837	Black American	809	Yes
66582	P.I.E.	Houston	TX	$13,992,714	Black American, Hispanic American	1,403	No
67910	MARTIN LUTHER KING	Houston	TX	$349,997	Black American	433	No
68529	LIGHT COMMERCE	Houston	TX	$2,595,191	Black American	785	Yes
24532	COVENANT SAVINGS	Killeen	TX	$2,656,360	Black American	1,378	Yes
1879	KINGSVILLE COMMUNITY	Kingsville	TX	$13,626,068	Hispanic American	1,877	Yes
15117	KINGSVILLE AREA EDUCATORS	Kingsville	TX	$18,765,419	Hispanic American	3,205	Yes
14734	LA JOYA AREA	La Joya	TX	$48,732,623	Hispanic American	16,609	Yes
16813	CAPROCK	Lamesa	TX	$28,580,162	Hispanic American	3,070	Yes
7024	SOUTH TEXAS REGIONAL	Laredo	TX	$6,895,072	Hispanic American	1,304	Yes
11011	LAREDO	Laredo	TX	$125,365,101	Hispanic American	18,149	Yes
12472	LAREDO FIRE DEPARTMENT	Laredo	TX	$11,153,024	Hispanic American	1,227	Yes
67579	TEX MEX	Laredo	TX	$13,023,854	Hispanic American	2,802	Yes
10776	TEACHERS ALLIANCE	Longview	TX	$1,532,482	Black American	406	Yes
8237	SOUTH TEXAS	McAllen	TX	$45,169,915	Hispanic American	7,549	Yes
67642	MTCU	Midland	TX	$105,850,943	Asian American, Black American, Hispanic American	8,477	No
14166	COCHRAN COUNTY SCHOOLS	Morton	TX	$4,649,505	Black American, Hispanic American	692	Yes
60533	SOUTHWEST HERITAGE	Odessa	TX	$108,760,928	Hispanic American	8,778	Yes
67592	WEST TEXAS EDUCATORS	Odessa	TX	$52,723,013	Black American, Hispanic American	4,845	No
20267	FRIO COUNTY	Pearsall	TX	$5,763,345	Hispanic American	1,427	No
19962	CITY-COUNTY	Pecos	TX	$897,430	Hispanic American	408	Yes
4148	HIGHWAY DISTRICT 21	Pharr	TX	$40,937,794	Hispanic American	4,094	Yes
10994	NAFT	Pharr	TX	$68,999,256	Hispanic American	9,662	Yes

7023	PORT ARTHUR COMMUNITY	Port Arthur	TX	$18,100,212	Asian American, Black American, Hispanic American	2,392	Yes
2077	PRAIRIE VIEW	Prairie View	TX	$4,711,479	Black American	822	Yes
5935	COWBOY COUNTRY	Premont	TX	$13,282,393	Hispanic American	2,026	Yes
13765	QUEMADO	Quemado	TX	$1,426,498	Hispanic American	469	Yes
6012	BLUE CROSS TEXAS	Richardson	TX	$38,832,425	Asian American, Black American, Hispanic American	4,199	No
18559	STARR COUNTY TEACHERS	Rio Grande City	TX	$25,725,267	Hispanic American	5,010	Yes
926	RIVER CITY	San Antonio	TX	$131,376,845	Hispanic American	14,569	Yes
2825	DIVISION 694 MOTOR COACH EMP	San Antonio	TX	$2,696,538	Black American, Hispanic American	1,420	Yes
2995	ALAMO	San Antonio	TX	$43,918,866	Hispanic American	6,329	Yes
3064	SELECT	San Antonio	TX	$33,472,882	Hispanic American	5,445	Yes
4015	GENERATIONS COMMUNITY	San Antonio	TX	$514,441,671	Asian American, Black American, Hispanic American	48,571	Yes
10913	SOUTHWEST RESEARCH CENTER	San Antonio	TX	$69,566,356	Hispanic American	10,156	Yes
12200	SAN ANTONIO WATER SYSTEM	San Antonio	TX	$2,777,227	Hispanic American	1,082	Yes
15973	EXPRESS-NEWS	San Antonio	TX	$6,685,071	Hispanic American	1,294	Yes
23184	TEXAS ASSOCIATIONS OF PROFESSIONALS	San Antonio	TX	$28,132,078	Hispanic American	2,694	No
61267	TEXAS WORKFORCE	San Antonio	TX	$9,648,210	Hispanic American	1,227	No
24384	NIZARI PROGRESSIVE	Sugar Land	TX	$103,313,434	Asian American	10,797	No
24818	PIONEER MUTUAL	Sugar Land	TX	$96,304,943	Asian American	7,113	No
15112	STONE TYLER EMPLOYEES	Tyler	TX	$106,035	Black American, Hispanic American	32	Yes
5555	WACONIZED	Waco	TX	$4,755,322	Black American	490	Yes
Total No. of Minority Depository Institutions for Texas: 96				**$8,569,890,215**		**1,165,323**	

UTAH MINORITY DEPOSITORY INSTITUTIONS

CHARTER	NAME	CITY	STATE	ASSETS	MINORITY TYPE	MEMBERS	LOW INCOME
67163	SAN JUAN	Blanding	UT	$15,450,302	Native American	4,200	Yes
67005	NATIONAL J. A. C. L.	Salt Lake City	UT	$31,707,441	Asian American	4,133	No
Total No. of Minority Depository Institutions for Utah: 2				**$47,157,743**		**8,333**	

VIRGINIA MINORITY DEPOSITORY INSTITUTIONS

CHARTER	NAME	CITY	STATE	ASSETS	MINORITY TYPE	MEMBERS	LOW INCOME
1407	HEW	Alexandria	VA	$159,539,173	Black American	18,537	Yes
24640	MOUNT PLEASANT BAPTIST CHURCH	Alexandria	VA	$149,689	Black American	132	No
16172	QUEEN OF PEACE ARLINGTON	Arlington	VA	$2,390,992	Asian American, Black American, Hispanic American	447	Yes
13032	DINWIDDIE EDUCATION ASSOC	Dinwiddie	VA	$1,695,515	Black American	278	No

66950	HAMPTON CITY EMP CREDIT UNION INC.	Hampton	VA	$5,705,464	Black American	1,842	No
24281	MOSAIC	Harrisonburg	VA	$13,332,959	Hispanic American	3,782	Yes
10636	BRUNSWICK COUNTY TEACHERS	Lawrenceville	VA	$804,494	Black American	420	Yes
19416	GLAMORGAN EMPLOYEES	Lynchburg	VA	$961,820	Black American	233	No
22049	PORT OF HAMPTON ROADS ILA	Norfolk	VA	$6,489,777	Black American	1,722	Yes
66896	PETERSBURG FED REF CREDIT UNION INC	North Prince GE	VA	$4,055,436	Black American	743	No
4833	PORTSMOUTH SCHOOLS	Portsmouth	VA	$2,322,672	Black American	1,500	Yes
16970	PORTSMOUTH VA CITY EMPLOYEES	Portsmouth	VA	$2,162,845	Black American	876	Yes
23114	NEW BETHEL	Portsmouth	VA	$111,476	Black American	176	Yes
1282	RICHMOND HERITAGE	Richmond	VA	$6,959,412	Black American	2,344	Yes
24616	TBC	Richmond	VA	$130,165	Black American	184	Yes
60111	CADMUS CREDIT UNION INCORPORATED	Richmond	VA	$2,174,430	Black American	649	No
66929	THE RICHMOND POSTAL CREDIT UNION IN	Richmond	VA	$78,273,875	Black American	7,343	No
11986	HIGH STREET BAPTIST CHURCH	Roanoke	VA	$1,824,296	Black American	323	Yes
23760	HALIFAX COUNTY COMMUNITY	South Boston	VA	$7,026,549	Black American	5,370	Yes
3029	VIRGINIA STATE UNIVERSITY	South Chesterfield	VA	$9,893,370	Black American	2,303	Yes
5970	METROPOLITAN CHURCH	Suffolk	VA	$7,696,205	Black American	1,820	No
21367	PLANTERS	Suffolk	VA	$4,032,930	Black American	881	Yes
24535	FIRST BAPTIST CHURCH OF VIENNA (VA)	Vienna	VA	$1,425,878	Black American	411	No
Total No. of Minority Depository Institutions for Virginia: 23				**$319,159,422**		**52,316**	

U.S. VIRGIN ISLANDS MINORITY DEPOSITORY INSTITUTIONS

CHARTER	NAME	CITY	STATE	ASSETS	MINORITY TYPE	MEMBERS	LOW INCOME
7970	ST. THOMAS	Charlotte Amalie	VI	$51,024,737	Black American	6,528	Yes
23294	VITELCO EMPLOYEES	Charlotte Amalie	VI	$2,232,104	Black American	427	Yes
7989	CHRISTIANSTED	Christiansted	VI	$21,904,163	Black American	3,707	Yes
23811	MID-ISLAND	Christiansted	VI	$8,642,737	Black American	2,474	Yes
8069	FREDERIKSTED	Frederiksted	VI	$11,399,003	Black American	2,684	Yes
Total No. of Minority Depository Institutions for the U.S. Virgin Islands: 5				**$95,202,744**		**15,820**	

WASHINGTON MINORITY DEPOSITORY INSTITUTIONS

CHARTER	NAME	CITY	STATE	ASSETS	MINORITY TYPE	MEMBERS	LOW INCOME
12281	NORTHWEST BAPTIST	Seattle	WA	$4,605,815	Black American	951	Yes

| 68304 | LOWER VALLEY | Sunnyside | WA | $67,772,279 | Hispanic American | 9,637 | Yes |

Total No. of Minority Depository Institutions for Washington: 2 — **$72,378,094** — **10,588**

WEST VIRGINIA MINORITY DEPOSITORY INSTITUTIONS

CHARTER	NAME	CITY	STATE	ASSETS	MINORITY TYPE	MEMBERS	LOW INCOME
68112	W. VIRGINIA STATE CONVENTION	Hilltop	WV	$195,292	Black American	146	Yes

Total No. of Minority Depository Institutions for West Virginia: 1 — **$195,292** — **146**

WISCONSIN MINORITY DEPOSITORY INSTITUTIONS

CHARTER	NAME	CITY	STATE	ASSETS	MINORITY TYPE	MEMBERS	LOW INCOME
24648	LCO	Hayward	WI	$1,811,995	Native American	1,621	Yes
66806	GREATER GALILEE BAPTIST	Milwaukee	WI	$196,236	Black American	118	Yes
68044	HOLY REDEEMER COMMUNITY OF SE WIS.	Milwaukee	WI	$855,749	Black American	278	Yes
68533	CTK	Milwaukee	WI	$165,922	Black American	350	Yes

Total No. of Minority Depository Institutions for Wisconsin: 4 — **$3,029,902** — **2,367**

Total No. of Minority Depository Institutions : 688 — **$36,907,162,097** — **4,536,783**

Appendix 2: Charter Enhancements to Minority Depository Institutions

APPROVED NEW LOW-INCOME DESIGNATION TO MINORITY DEPOSITORY INSTITUTIONS

State	City	Charter	Name	Date Approved
CA	Los Angeles	68459	USC	8/21/2013
CT	Fairfield	24723	Fairfield County	10/18/2013
GA	Suwanee	24234	Omega Psi Phi Frater	12/2/2013
IL	Chicago	62497	Maroon Financial	9/3/2013
IL	Waukegan	15812	Shiloh Baptist	3/25/2014
IL	Zion	67024	Mt. Zion	4/1/2014
KY	Louisville	61316	Tarcana	3/19/2014
LA	Lake Charles	62756	Southwest Louisiana	6/19/2014
MD	Baltimore	2769	SecurityPlus	7/1/2013
MI	Detroit	60993	Metropolitan Church of God	1/27/2014
MN	Nett Lake	24852	Northern Eagle	10/10/2013
MO	Kansas City	61459	Cross Roads	7/11/2013
NJ	Elizabeth	22032	Entertainment Industries	9/12/2013
NJ	Hamilton	1546	Mercer County Improvement Authority	5/7/2014
OH	Toledo	21226	Promedica	4/16/2014
SC	West Columbia	24623	Brookland	11/21/2013
TX	Dallas	68436	New Mount Zion Baptist Church	6/10/2014
TX	El Paso	5929	Tip of Texas	5/9/2014
VA	Arlington	16172	Queen of Peace Arlington	11/19/2013
WV	Hilltop	68112	W. Virginia State Convention	5/19/2014

Total Minority Depository Institutions: 20

APPROVED NEW CHARTER TO MINORITY DEPOSITORY INSTITUTIONS

State	City	Charter	Name	Date Approved
MN	Nett Lake	24852	Northern Eagle	10/10/2013

Total Minority Depository Institutions: 1

APPROVED COMMUNITY CHARTER CONVERSION TO MINORITY DEPOSITORY INSTITUTIONS

State	City	Charter	Name	Date Approved
HI	Kahului	2562	Maui	8/16/2013

Total Minority Depository Institutions: 1

Appendix 3: Grants and Loans to Minority Depository Institutions

LOANS TO MINORITY DEPOSITORY INSTITUTIONS

State	City	Charter	Name	Loan Amount
TX	Del Rio	24304	Border	$500,000
TX	Houston	15817	Pilgrim CUCC	$150,000
TX	San Antonio	3064	Select	$500,000
Total Minority Depository Institutions: 3				**$1,150,000**

URGENT NEED GRANTS TO MINORITY DEPOSITORY INSTITUTIONS

State	City	Charter	Name	Initiative Awarded	Grant Amount
HI	Pepeekeo	2280	Hamakua Coast Community	Building Repairs	$7,500
IL	Waukegan	24614	Gideon	Hardware/Equipment	$648
OH	Toledo	68603	Nueva Esperanza Community	Hardware/Equipment	$6,085
PA	Philadelphia	14430	Wesley AME Zion	Building Repairs	$7,500
Total Minority Depository Institutions: 4					**$21,732**

GRANTS TO MINORITY DEPOSITORY INSTITUTIONS

State	City	Charter	Name	Initiative Awarded	Grant Amount
AR	Pine Bluff	7700	Arkansas AM&N College	Student Internship	$2,000
CA	Pomona	14739	Cal Poly	Student Internship	$4,000
CA	Santa Cruz	64029	Santa Cruz Community	New Product/ Financial Capability	$12,469
CA	Soledad	13254	Corrections	Student Internship	$4,000
CO	Alamosa	63468	Valley Educators	Staff and Training	$2,990
CO	Antonito	65471	Guadalupe Parish	New Product	$15,000
CO	Las Animas	1479	Arkansas Valley	Staff and Training	$2,395
CT	Bridgeport	23896	East End Baptist Tabernacle	Financial Capability	$5,000
DC	Washington	538	Government Printing Office	New Product	$14,500
DC	Washington	20377	Peoples-Neighborhood	Staff and Training/ New Product	$9,040
DE	Wilmington	24845	Stepping Stones Community	Financial Capability	$10,000
FL	Miami	14391	Baptist Health South Florida	New Product	$6,000
FL	West Palm Beach	16834	Town of Palm Beach	New Product	$3,100

GA	Augusta	14103	Tabernacle	New Product	$1,200
GA	Suwanee	24234	Omega Psi Phi Fraternity	Student Internship	$4,000
HI	Hilo	1607	Big Island	New Product	$8,000
HI	Hilo	5628	Independent Employers Group	Staff and Training	$1,750
HI	Honolulu	5099	The Queen's	New Product	$2,080
HI	Honolulu	9115	Hotel And Travel Industry	New Product	$12,840
HI	Pepeekeo	2280	Hamakua Coast Community	Staff and Training	$2,193
IL	Aurora	63286	Fox Valley	CDFI Certification	$2,500
IL	Chicago	15673	Israel Methcomm	New Product/ Student Internship	$7,400
IL	Chicago	24188	Cosmopolitan	Student Internship	$4,000
IN	Fort Wayne	24781	Union Baptist Church	Staff and Training	$3,000
IN	Indianapolis	15757	Mt Zion Indianapolis	Student Internship	$2,750
LA	Alexandria	12225	Rapides	New Product	$1,365
LA	Jennings	14537	James Ward, Jr.	Student Internship	$3,000
LA	Minden	22219	U B C Southern Council Industrial WO	Staff and Training/ New Product	$3,650
LA	New Orleans	5839	Southeast Louisiana Veterans Health	New Product	$12,500
LA	New Orleans	12748	Xavier University	Student Internship	$4,000
LA	New Orleans	65659	Michoud	Student Internship	$4,000
LA	Plaquemine	12356	Iberville	Staff and Training	$389
MN	Mahnomen	17749	White Earth Reservation	Student Internship	$4,000
MO	Saint Louis	60400	St. Louis Community	New Product / Financial Capability	$16,439
MS	Jackson	24829	Hope	New Product	$14,500
NC	Durham	24802	Self-Help	Financial Capability	$5,000
NJ	Somerset	68195	Renaissance Community Development C	New Product	$6,800
NJ	Totowa	1015	North Jersey	CDFI Certification	$2,500
NM	Mora	62289	St. Gertrude's	Student Internship	$4,000
NM	Questa	66252	Questa	Home Banking	$10,000
NY	Long Island City	24823	Urban Upbound	Staff and Training/ Student Internship	$7,000
NY	New York	22032	Entertainment Industries	CDFI Certification	$2,500
NY	New York	23958	New York University	Student Internship	$4,000
NY	New York	24232	Lower East Side People's	New Product	$15,000
NY	Oakland Gardens	22344	Queens Cluster	Staff and Training	$1,500
NY	Ossining	4441	Sing Sing Employees	Bill Pay	$5,000
PA	Philadelphia	21535	The Triumph Baptist	Staff and Training	$1,200

SC	Orangeburg	1397	Edisto	New Product	$15,000
SC	West Columbia	24623	Brookland	Student Internship	$4,000
SD	Kyle	24847	Lakota	Staff and Training	$3,000
TX	El Paso	10174	Firstlight	New Product/ Financial Capability	$9,760
TX	Galveston	11927	Coastal Community	CDFI Certification	$2,500
TX	Houston	15817	Pilgrim CUCC	Student Internship	$4,000
TX	Houston	17067	Our Mother of Mercy Parish Houston	Student Internship	$4,000
TX	Houston	24463	Brentwood Baptist Church	Student Internship	$4,000
TX	Kingsville	1879	Kingsville Community	Staff and Training/ Student Internship	$7,000
TX	Lamesa	16813	Caprock	CDFI Certification	$2,500
TX	Morton	14166	Cochran County Schools	Student Internship	$4,000
TX	Pharr	10994	NAFT	Electronic, Digital Signatures	$6,000
TX	Port Arthur	7023	Port Arthur Community	Bill Pay	$5,000
VA	South Boston	23760	Halifax County Community	Student Internship	$3,420
VA	South Chesterfi	3029	Virginia State University	Student Internship	$4,000
VA	Suffolk	21367	Planters	New Product	$15,000
VI	Christiansted	23811	Mid-Island	Student Internship	$4,000
VI	Frederiksted	8069	Frederiksted	Student Internship	$4,000
WA	Sunnyside	68304	Lower Valley	New Product	$438
WI	Hayward	24648	LCO	Student Internship	$4,000
Total Minority Depository Institutions: 67					**$376,168**